AGENCY AND COMPANY

SAGE HUMAN SERVICES GUIDES, VOLUME 18

SAGE HUMAN SERVICES GUIDES

a series of books edited by ARMAND LAUFFER and published in cooperation with the Continuing Education Program in the Human Services of the University of Michigan School of Social Work.

A **SAGE** HUMAN SERVICES GUIDE **18**

AGENCY
AND COMPANY
Partners in
Human Resource
Development

Louis A. FERMAN
Roger MANELA
David ROGERS

Published in cooperation with
the Continuing Education Program in the Human Services
of the University of Michigan School of Social Work

SAGE PUBLICATIONS   Beverly Hills   London

For information address:

SAGE Publications, Inc.
275 South Beverly Drive
Beverly Hills, California 90212

SAGE Publications Ltd
28 Banner Street
London EC1Y 8QE, England

Printed in the United States of America

Library of Congress Cataloging in Publication Data

Ferman, Louis A
  Agency and company.

  (A Sage human service guide ; 18)
    1. Employees, Training of. 2. Hard-core
unemployed. 3. Subcontracting. 4. Interorganiza-
tional relations. I. Manela, Roger, joint author.
II. Rogers, David, 1930-   joint author.
III. Title.
HF5549.5.T7F39   658.3'24   80-23246
ISBN 0-8039-1558-6

FIRST PRINTING

CONTENTS

INTRODUCTION

Agency-company relations are at the core of effective employment and training programs for the disadvantaged and hard-to-employ. You will find this guide useful if you are:

- a director of a training and employment program
- a human service program planner
- a training director or supervisor
- a job developer responsible for establishing working relationships between agencies and companies
- an agency program developer who is establishing a joint company-agency program
- a company executive dealing with human service agencies for the delivery of some specific service.

Although our focus is on the joint agency-company development of human resource services for the hard-to-employ workers, the content of this guide may be applied to other human service areas in which an agency and a company seek to cooperate: mental health, general counseling, and alcoholism and drug abuse treatment. Our recommendations are based on extensive research on effective practices and reflect the collective wisdom of many experienced human resource practitioners.

We will explore the range of agency-company relationships, the conditions which make these relationships possible, and the manner by which they further or impede human resource programs. Contact between employer and the agency is viewed as a series of exchanges in which both organizations engage in voluntary activity between themselves for the realization of their respective goals and objectives—the agency as service deliverer, the company as consumer of those services. Companies supply agencies with job orders and agencies refer their clients to these job slots. Companies encounter problems in turnover and agencies provide supportive services—special counseling or replacement options. Companies require special orientation programs for their hard-to-employ workers and the agencies respond by organizing such programs.

In all of these exchange relationships, the company and agency seek to achieve certain benefits that are complementary: the agency by enlarging the opportunity structure for its clientele, the company by recruiting and developing a more efficient labor force. It is our thesis that such mutual benefits are at the center of successful agency-company relationships and once such benefits are no longer realized, or become one-sided, the relationship becomes unstable or terminates altogether. In practice, both organizations have accounting systems, explicit or implicit, where benefits from working relationships are continuously under review. This review may be affected by such factors as the "track record" of the clients in the company, the quality of service provided by the agency, and changes in the availability of labor supply in the labor market.

Our intention is to examine the complexity of agency-company relationships, to develop and present a useful framework for analysis of this activity that goes beyond the experience of any single agency, and to describe practical procedures and alternative strategies for conducting relations between agency and company. We caution the reader that some of the data, and indeed some of the interpretations, are tentative and reflect the present extent of knowledge in the area of agency-company relationships.

While this guide presents more than a description of the nature and extent of such relationships, it does not focus on the measurement of their effectiveness or impact on employment and training programs. This would presuppose standardization of agency activity and require a large number of situations where systematic assessment of this activity could be made. Such circumstances prevail only where extensive experience and a history of activity have allowed clear definition of objectives, standardization of procedures, and the development of criteria for judging outcomes. The practice of agency-company relations as a self-conscious and unique activity is too new, too innovative, and too changeable for such conditions and precludes precise measurement at this time.

In addition, the study of agency-company relations is itself a new undertaking and is still too undeveloped to use sophisticated measurement tools. We are at a stage where knowledge of such relationships is only now emerging in sufficient detail to suggest procedures for conducting them. As yet, agency personnel are still working on a trial-and-error basis. Energy is often invested to see what works, to discover what resources must be developed, and to decide where one set of practices and arrangements is better than another. In most cases, thinking about agency-company relations has been restricted to developing a single strategy for all situations. Seldom has any attempt been made to analyze the wide range of alternative strategies that do exist.

This guide is an amalgam of concepts from social science literature and ideas suggested by agency personnel, company officials, and our researchers. It specifies what we would consider good practice in developing agency-company relationships and suggests alternative reasons and techniques for developing such relationships. Even when these hypotheses lack strong empirical support, they can act as reference points for practitioners and future research. We try to analyze why some procedures are more or less desirable than others.

We would like to acknowledge the help and advice of a large number of practitioners who made valuable suggestions in the development of this manuscript. John C Erfurt, our colleague, read an initial draft of the manuscript and a number of his insights have been incorporated into the text. I would like to thank Maralyn Jennings, who typed several versions of this manuscript.

We would particularly like to thank Armand Lauffer for the assistance he rendered in editing the material and for his encouragement throughout the process of writing this guide.

Chapter 1

PERSPECTIVES ON AGENCY-COMPANY RELATIONSHIPS

The private company is a vital element in operations for the hard-to-employ. First and foremost, it provides jobs for the clients in the many training and prevocational programs. Second, it provides the hard day-to-day experiences in the world of work where the client is expected to translate his agency training and learning into action. Third, it gives some legitimacy to the agency program by being a supporter of that program through using it. Finally, it is a consumer of the various service programs that the agency develops to facilitate the placement of the hard-to-employ job applicant.

Important challenges are inherent in the interactions between agency and company.

First, the agency must gain *access* to the company and win its cooperation. Basic considerations include the appeal of the agency's services to the company, the competition to the agency posed by other public and private agencies, and the image and reputation of the particular agency and of employment and training programs generally.

Second, environmental factors, such as the state of the labor market or changing corporate attitudes toward social responsibility, affect the degree and durability of agency-company relationships. The agency may have easy access to a company in placing clients in a tight labor market but be rebuffed when the market "softens."

Third, the relationship is under continuous examination because the agency and the company have unequal power and influence. The agency must initiate contact while the opportunity to respond lies with the company and is subject to continuous bargaining and negotiations.

Fourth, the agency and the company have different organizational goals and philosophies. The agency is concerned with successful placements of clients while the company's primary interest lies in the contribution that such clients can have *as workers* in the company.

These challenges, which have not confronted the agency in the past, require new planning with an emphasis on professional training, resources, and personnel.

AGENCY OPERATIONS

Five types of service delivery operations can be conducted between an agency and a company.

PURE JOB PLACEMENT

Pure job placement consists of filling employment requests made by the company to the agency. There is no attempt to change the applicant by giving him skills and attitudes that will make him more suitable for a specific job order and there is no attempt to change the demands of the company to meet agency supply.

JOB PLACEMENT INVOLVING APPLICANT MODIFICATION

Some job placement activities often require modifying the skills and attitudes of the job applicant, both to improve his employability and fit the requirements of the job order.

JOB CREATION

Job creation involves the manipulation of the labor market to create new job opportunities. For example, the agency can prompt the employer to undertake contracts providing resources for upgrading employed workers. The agency may seek to sponsor enlarged employment in the company by serving as a broker to obtain loans or grants for industrial expansion. Or the agency may supply technical expertise for job redesign or manpower development, which result in new job opportunities for the hard-to-employ.

JOB DEVELOPMENT

Job development as we use the term involves the modification of company entrance requirements and work practices regarding the hard-to-employ. This cannot be successful without competence in the three above-mentioned areas. In effect, job development is the combination and interaction of pure job placement, applicant modification, and job creation. Success here opens the door to a more sophisticated approach to job development—one which emphasizes large-scale revision of employment structures. This, in turn, results in more meaningful job opportunities for the hard-to-employ, a system of supportive services for new workers, and development of an organization that seeks to create job opportunities by eliminating traditional barriers to employment.

EMPLOYER MANPOWER SYSTEM DEVELOPMENT

Employer manpower system development involves working with companies to create permanent structures within which the company will be more receptive to the hiring, training, and development of the hard-to-employ. This type of agency involves itself in the employer's Human Resource Development program.

Which of these operations is conducted depends on a number of factors, including the objectives of the relationship, employer need, agency mandate and resources, and staff ability. What does not vary, however, is the way in which the relationship between the agency and the employer occurs—the process it follows.

THE SYSTEM OF HUMAN RESOURCE OPERATIONS

A system of human resource operations consists of three basic elements:

(1) the job or client applicant
(2) the employment and training agency
(3) the company.

As a link between hard-to-employ job seekers and private companies, the strategies and operation of the employment and training agency must be directed toward two client groups: the job applicant and the employer. Working with companies requires not only intelligence about the company (e.g., how corporate decisions are made) but also information on what the job applicant seeks and wants in the world of work. In a similar fashion, the company must come to understand the capabilities and limitations of the agency services and the needs of the job seekers who are referred.

The hard-to-employ job seeker will be evaluated quite differently by agency and company personnel. Agency personnel will assess him in terms of his *career performance* and ask such questions as: What is the quality of his current job situation compared to the situation that he faced before he sought agency services? To what extent has the job in the company lived up to the promises made by management and permitted the job seeker to achieve personal goals and needs in employment? Has the job seeker moved up the mobility ladder or reached a dead end?

Company personnel will assess the job candidate in terms of his *job* performance. How does his productivity compare to others? Has he been a disciplined worker or is he a behavior problem? To what extent does he give signs of meeting management criteria for job performance? These differences in evaluation criteria stem from the fact that to agency personnel the job seeker is a *client* who seeks services to improve his life situation while to the company he is an *employee* who seeks to make a contribution to the productivity of his organization. Working relationships between agency and company will involve, then, mutual recognition of the job seeker's needs and motivations in his dual role as a recipient of agency services and as a jobholder.

Agencies can provide a number of services to companies: recruitment of manpower; financial incentives for hiring agency clients; prevocational or upgrading programs for unskilled workers; and technical assistance in testing, counseling, and developing applications for government subsidy assistance. The main services that the agency offers to the job applicant are to determine his job aspirations, expand his capabilities through training, place him in a suitable work position, and provide temporary follow-up to deal with any problems that may arise on the job. The agency tries to match his skills and preferences to the available job openings. After placement, the agency tries to retain contact with the applicant to help him adjust to the job situation and act as a communication link with company personnel to facilitate solution of any complaints or problems. If the initial placement does not work out, the agency may well attempt to relocate the applicant. This is a comprehensive picture of agency-client services, but individual agencies may stress one or another service or not provide some of them.

Simply stated, the employment and training agency is in business to place hard-to-employ job applicants in job openings which provide an opportunity for them to earn a reasonable living and develop a career. This most basic goal is not easily achieved when employers are reluctant to hire certain categories of job applicants or when the jobs available do not offer careers with any future. In such situations, the agency must go beyond the mere filling of available job orders and seek to expand or create employment opportunities. In order to achieve these objectives, employment and training agencies must engage in a number of different kinds of relationships with employers.

THE SEVEN STAGES OF THE
AGENCY-COMPANY RELATIONSHIP

In the following discussion we will view the agency-company relationship as a seven-stage process. It begins with an analysis of the resources that an agency requires to gain *access* to a company and ends with the steps that must be taken to *disengage* from a company once, the decision is made to terminate the relationship. The seven stages, briefly summarized, are as follows:

(1) *Access*—This involves the strategy of approaching a company; gaining the information and sponsorship needed. Who should be contacted and the characteristics of effective initial contact situations will be discussed.

(2) Engagement—Once into a company, diagnosis of company problems and promises must be made. We will describe how a base of support can be built for the service program.

(3) *Negotiating an Agreement*—Somewhere along the line, the company's commitment for service must be translated into written agreement. The actual written agreement is preceded by negotiations between both parties. Principles that inform effective negotiations are discussed.

(4) *Program Development*—The actual administration and organization of service delivery requires choices among options. The components of effective program development in companies are outlined.

(5) *Maintenance*—A working relationship must be nurtured. This requires extensive staff work by both company and agency personnel. We will suggest tasks to be performed by each.

(6) *Assessment*—At a number of points, the relationship must be reviewed, assessed, and analyzed. This involves a sorting and sifting of data from a variety of sources that we will describe.

(7) *Disengagement*—The decision to withdraw or terminate the relationship involves both the gathering of information and interactions between agency and company personnel. We will suggest how this can be done in the best interests of the client.

Agency-company relationships, then, are viewed as a number of interrelated stages in a process. These stages are probably not as tightly compartmentalized as we have indicated. They overlap and a number of them may coexist at any given point in time. Our sequencing of stages begins with an analysis of the resources that an agency requires to gain access to a company; moves on to a consideration of who is to be seen in the company to cement the commitments for service; is followed by a consideration of how programs and service delivery systems of the agency are developed and stabilized; and concludes with the decision that service delivery to the company is complete and withdrawal should follow. This perspective permits us to view agency-company relationships in terms of a number of related decision points.

Each of the chapters, 2 through 8, focuses on one of the seven stages of the agency-company relationship. We conclude each of the chapters with a summary of items that should characterize *your* agency efforts in a particular stage of the relationship.

In the Appendix, we look at the two critical roles in a human resource agency that are involved in the development and maintenance of agency-company relationships.[1] First, *Agency Administrators* are charged with the direction of the agency's service program as well as overseeing the coordination of other agency staff efforts in achieving agency goals and objectives. Second, *Job Developers* have the responsibility for developing or finding job openings as well as helping to remove company barriers to the placement of agency clients.

For both roles, we look at the tasks and responsibilities required within and across the seven stages of the agency-company relationship. We present a series of practice principles which specify how administrators and job developers ideally participate during the course of agency-company relationships in terms of:

(1) operational objectives for the particular role

(2) activities to be carried out

(3) strategies to be used

(4) decisions to be considered

(5) resources needed.

These principles reflect the best judgment of practitioners on how to make agency-company relationships work. After reading each chapter of the guide, the reader should turn and read the corresponding material in the Appendix to see what *should be done* by administrators and job developers to operationalize a particular stage.

By presenting the material in this way, the reader can make use of this document in two different ways: (1) as a guide to what is necessary for the *agency* to do at each stage of the agency-company relationship and (2) as a guide to the practice principles that are required for both administrators and job developers involved in the relationship.

N O T E

1. Other staff members—trainers, supervisors, program developers, and planners—may perform any or all of the tasks described in this guide. Agency-company relationships are team efforts. The ways you design your team and the ways in which tasks are assigned in your organization are up to you. We think you will find our suggestions on target. We would like your feedback. Please complete the evaluation form at the end of the guide so that we can improve the next edition of the guide.

Chapter 2

ACCESS:
Approaching the Company

Gaining entry into a company is not only the first step for the agency but also it may well be the most important. Important questions about access include the following:

- How are target companies selected?
- What information should be used?
- How should sponsorship systems be used?
- How should influence systems be used?
- How should company development responsibilities be assigned?
- What are the characteristics of the first contact?
- What are effective appeal strategies?

"Forget Industrial Tire," Charlie Tobin advised. "They've never been interested in the hard-to-employ." "That may be," agreed Cathy Marshall, assistant director of JOB, Inc., deferring to her boss. "But I think their situation may be different today. The NAB people [Local Chapter of the National Alliance of Businessmen] tell me that there's a new management team over there, and some instruction from the home office that they have to improve their community image. Last year's recall orders and the flak over their pollution controls really did them in. I think they may be ripe for some kind of community service. It may not be much, but it could be an opening. Do you think I should call them?" "No, I'm not convinced. Let's give Ed Watkins at NAB a call and ask him to test the water for us."

Gaining access to the company consists of two steps.

STEP 1: PRECONTACT OPERATIONS

Extensive work must be done before the actual initial contacts between agency and company personnel. The target companies must be selected. There must be some planning and assignment of agency personnel to work with company personnel. Sponsorship of the agency into the companies must be developed and arranged. Information on the companies must be gathered. All of these require careful planning with specific objectives, an assignment of agency personnel, and some mechanisms to measure success and/or failure.

HOW ARE TARGET COMPANIES SELECTED?

At first it would seem that the large number of companies in any community would be a sufficient market for agency services. Processes of selection, however, must limit this pool of potential users. Selection of target companies may vary from well-defined, systematic market selection procedures to acting on tips and contacts. Some agencies set up a schedule of industries within which to work and specified companies of a certain size to be contacted. Selection processes are highly programmed and structured. Other agencies rely on informal leads developed through contacts with the business community.

Principle: Develop Informal Employer Contacts

In each agency some time and resources of staff, including administrators, must be invested in developing informal contacts with business executives in a variety of settings.

In these settings, a case for the agency program can be made and "recruits" solicited who could communicate the message to other companies. These informal contacts also become excellent sources of information on company "trouble spots" that may need agency services as well as sources of sponsorship of the agency program in the company. Have the agency represented at trade association meetings, local Chamber of Commerce meetings, and by membership in professional business associations and conferences with key business leaders.

There are three patterns of company selection:

(1) *self-selection* where the company refers itself to the agency for some service
(2) *planned selection* where the agency uses specific criteria to include some companies and by-pass others
(3) *fortuitous selection* where the company becomes a target either through chance or because some relationship has existed in the past and is now actively exploited.

Each type of selection has its strengths and weaknesses. The companies which come to the agency appear desirable because they are motivated by some need to seek the agency service. They do not have to be sold on the value of the service. The drawback is that such companies have definite but limited service requests. From the beginning the agency's inputs are restricted to the specific problem at hand.

In planned selection, it is assumed that the agency will define target companies in terms of company problems that can be treated by its available service. Obviously, this all assumes that relevant data on the company are available to the agency. Without such data, the criteria may be meaningless.

In the case of fortuitous selection, the choice is based on chance factors (e.g., accidental informal contacts with company executives) or past service relationships. Accidental, informal contacts are limited by their unpredictability. Nevertheless, the number of such contacts can be increased if the agency takes steps to develop channels to management centers. Attendance or representation at trade association meetings; active participation in the local Chamber of Commerce; membership in professional business organizations; and regular contacts with key business leaders have the potential of presenting and diffusing the agency's case.

Capitalizing on past relationships to establish new programs is certainly a sounder approach. Barriers in the company to future service delivery will be minimal once services have been received and used. Although this formulation is appealing, several problems exist. Past service relationships may give the company a restricted view of the agency's capabilities. The agency speciality of the past can create an organizational identity that will restrict the spread of services rather than encourage expansion for new program activity.

The purpose or content of the services will also affect the selection of target companies. In cases where a discrete service complements or supplements company practices or goals, the potential number of firms may be quite high. In other cases, where the company is being asked to modify existing policies or practices, the demand will be considerably lower. Services to a company may fall into three categories:

(1) those designed to expand a given company activity without modification or change in practices

(2) those that seek to modify a given company activity (e.g., new counseling inputs or modified hiring/promotion standards)

(3) those that seek to develop innovations or new structures that have not existed before. The number of companies that are receptive to such innovations is usually small, although some companies do have an organizational tradition of promoting innovations.

The case example we used at the beginning of this chapter may be used to illustrate the point. New directives from the home office to modify the company's local image set the stage for a new penetration effort by the human resource agency. But in and of itself, this would not have been sufficient inducement.

"Tell you what," suggested Watkins from NAB, "let me do some checking. I'm having lunch with one of the new managers at Industrial Tire next week. I've heard that they've had some difficulties in keeping people on the job in section C operations. The pay is low and the work is dull. It may not be much, but it may be a place to start—especially if you guys can give their foreman some help in restructuring the jobs and instruct them on coaching techniques like you did at McGraw Paper Mills."

A strategy for gaining access was in the beginning stage of formulation. A company was targeted for possible penetration. Its needs were identified, and the potential for providing the company with needed services was explored.

Potential target companies must be examined in the light of their receptivity to various service inputs. It goes without saying that the number of target companies may be increased by giving them the prerogative of choosing services. As we have already noted, the danger is that the agency may be reduced to a reactive role and the company may select services that have a minimal impact on the hiring and retaining of the hard-to-employ.

One other consideration in company selection should be noted. Some firms, such as restaurants and hotels, are so tightly linked to industrial or business associations that individual solicitation has little impact or meets great resistance. In these cases, it might make more sense to gain access to the association and through it to the target company; the agency will have a powerful ally to increase company receptivity and a number of potential target companies instead of one. This is particularly true if the service package is innovative.

WHAT INFORMATION SHOULD BE USED?

Before any selection system can operate, extensive information concerning a company's receptivity and possible resistance is required. Since many agencies lack a system to direct them to companies where their services may best be used, they frequently reach out blindly and take what they can in the way of company clients. Planned selection gives way to expediency and convenience. Consequently, selection criteria, if they exist, emphasize nonservice-related considerations—how prestigious the company is or how easy access is to the company.

Undoubtedly, the weakest link in the development of an agency-company relationship has been the *lack of preparation preceding the initial contact.* Cold solicitation in person or by telephone has not proven to be effective in selling job development as an operational concept to the employer. Five basic activities should precede the initial contact.

First, the agency personnel unit should make a thorough study of the structure of the industry, including manpower and technological trends, growth patterns, status of minority group employment, and previous experience with the hard-to-employ. It is particularly important to isolate key job areas that might be suitable (in their present form or by restructuring) for entry jobs. The identification of surplus employment or shortages in manpower should be explored in considerable detail.

Second, the target firm and its relationship to the industry should be analyzed. The following factors are particularly important: traditional sources of manpower, competitive position, growth/decline picture in earnings, technological development, and new product marketing. What may be more important than current job vacancies is the long-run potential of the company to create jobs and to restructure other jobs to give jobs to the hard-to-employ.

Third, the social structure of the firm should be identified, especially assumptions about employment and decision-making patterns. If the company views each job candidate in terms of a career rather than a job, the prospects for entry jobs may be diminished. Quite frequently, there is a tendency to talk to the wrong person, one who does not make the crucial decisions or have the influence to persuade others. One of the frequent problems in job development units is that the approach is to the front office personnel employee who does not set job standards or qualifications but merely acts to fill a prescribed job order. Change in this situation requires reaching back into the organization to the person or persons who actually decide what goes into the job order. This is frequently the department chief or a job analyst. The capacity for change is in these positions.

Fourth, previous experiences with inducing change in the company should be analyzed. It is particularly helpful to identify the strategies that led to change and the agents responsible for the change. This analysis will include a factoring of change agents within the firm as well as outside. What is being suggested here is the necessity to identify and use power modes that can affect change. Access to individuals and agencies that have had previous contact with the company can be a rich source of diagnosis in such problems. Job development involves an identification of change agents and the planned mobilization of resources and influences to induce changes in policy. The obvious inference is that to induce change, one must understand not only the firm's relations to the industry but also its relationship to the community power structure. Each firm is unique and the influences that effect change in one company may be ineffective in another.

Fifth, not only is it necessary to identify *who* shapes policy in *what manner* but also *how* the individual may be reached. These considerations range from the selection of a proper setting (for example, a working breakfast) to the selection of a proper strategy. Three points about strategy are worth noting. First, it must be clear that the job development logic should be broken down into basic operational points which avoid abstract rhetoric. It is important to present a plan adapted to the structure of this particular company, indicating points at which changes may be required or desirable. Second, the nature of the appeal must be adapted to the company context and to the individual contact. There may be times when normal persuasion is appropriate and other times when confrontation will be most appropriate. The selection of the appeal will depend on the extent to which the *weltanschauung* of the company has been absorbed in the diagnosis of company structure and philosophy. Finally, the selection of a specific strategy should be related to certain expected outcomes from the company contact. One strategy may be effective in bringing forth pledges for jobs and *promises* of cooperation, while another may be more influential in bringing forth *actual* commitments and an operational plan. It must be clear to the agency what the priorities and intended outcomes are in the situation. It goes without saying that these must be developed in considerable detail in the preparatory period.

Principle: *Continually update and supplement company information. Information should be gathered on:*

1. *Presently involved companies.* In order to improve and expand services, company-assigned staff should keep their eyes open for possibilities of developing job programs in other departments. Information concerning job openings, particularly those that offer advancement opportunities, is valuable.

2. *Unsuccessfully approached companies.* Companies that were not amenable to program involvement during the initial contact should not necessarily be dismissed entirely. Changes in management, policy, economic climates, and so on may alter this posture, providing an agency with door-opening possibilities.

3. *New potentially receptive companies.* The following sources of information should be tapped:

   a. *Reference documents.* Frequent use should be made of the A.G. Becker Guide, Dunn and Bradstreet Analytical Reports, and local industrial and manufacturer's directories, companies' fiscal reports, and public relations literature.

   b. *Business and industrial organizations.* The local chapter of the National Alliance of Businessmen (NAB) or the local Chamber of Commerce can be good sources.

c. *Other agency staff and associates.* Experienced staff, resource, and information components of an agency should be consulted.

d. *Others with an "inside" view of the company.* It may be possible to gain valuable information on the company by meeting after hours with a union steward in the company. Securing information from people who know the company intimately is excellent whenever possible, but often difficult.

Cathy Marshall has received the go-ahead to approach Industrial Tire. The "case" has been assigned to Lou Sherman, a newly hired job developer. "Who should I call at the company?" "Whoa," says Cathy, "there's a lot of work to do before we see anyone at the company. Let's get some basic information on the company first. Do your homework before you approach the company. Our agency has a file on Industrial Tire. Study it. You will want to talk to Ed Watkins who knows them well. Talk to anyone and everyone that you can lay hands on that knows anyone or anything about the company. Bill Jacobs, their personnel representative, has done a lot of work with employment agencies and he has been on our board. Keep in close touch with him; he can give you inside dope on who's who and what is happening in the company.

"Remember the rule—soften them up before you see them. That means getting some big-time operators in the community to put in a good word for you and the program first. The more, the better. There's a lot of work to do before you actually see anyone at the company."

HOW SHOULD SPONSORSHIP SYSTEMS BE USED?

Access may be enhanced through various sponsorship systems. We have already mentioned that target companies may be made available to the agency through a sponsoring organization and that company receptivity may be increased if business associations are enlisted as allies or sponsors. Some agencies have prestigious sponsors as integral parts of their organization. For other agencies, sponsorship must be developed. *Multiple sponsorship* reinforces the capacity of the agency to gain access to corporate structures.

One point deserves emphasis. Sponsorship can enhance your capacity to gain access to some companies but it may sharply limit the strategy alternatives open to the agency. Undoubtedly certain allies and activist tactics which could have been used to gain influence for an agency can be closed to it because of its association with a particular sponsor. Government-sponsored agencies have less freedom in strategy development than private agencies because of political considerations and because of the limitations imposed by legislation or regulation. Thus we see that sponsorship can both open and close channels of access.

In some kinds of sponsorship, the agency will be linked to legal systems of the company. Such is the case of Manpower agencies working closely with federal or state legal authorities (Civil Rights Commission, Equal Employment Opportunity Commission, and State Fair Employment Practices Commissions). This would seem to be a built-in access situation but it can only go so far since company resentments may well offset initial gains. The dominant form of access must still be through the mobilization of persuasion of influence systems.

HOW SHOULD INFLUENCE SYSTEMS BE USED?

An important consideration is the question of how much influence an agency can mobilize in seeking organizational access to a company. At one extreme, the agency can confine itself to persuasion or salesmanship in gaining access. At the other extreme, the agency can seek to exploit community resources, use other agencies, and develop coalitions and allies to gain access to companies. Between these extremes, attention can be given to the penetration and manipulation of influence channels within the company. Although persuasion and interpersonal relations are by far the most frequent forms of influence used, the potential of the other forms has been recognized and their use varies with circumstances.

The crucial factors are: the nature of the mandate the agency has, its organizational structure, and its kind of expertise. Many agencies feel constrained by the nature of their mandate and limit their influence attempts to persuasion, lest the company feel that it is being coerced or unduly pressured. Even agencies that recognize the legitimacy of coalition politics may preclude it as a strategy. In agencies where considerable time is invested in client processing or other procedures which stress intraagency obligations, there are just not enough resources (manpower, finances, or time) to invest in the systematic building of channels of influence that may or may not have some impact on company receptivity. But by far the most important barrier is a lack of expertise in developing such channels. Few agency staffs have this vital skill or make provisions for its acquisition.

Despite the lack of experience in its application, most agencies expect to exert either a direct influence on a company or use the pressure network of other organizations (resource organizations, consumer organizations, licensing organizations, unions, professional organizations, and manpower procurement organizations).

In recent years, some minority group organizations have begun to establish a measure of influence with companies. One should remember that companies like Industrial Tire are sensitive to public opinion and to certain reference publics (e.g., the black community). Thus, a sound strategy would be to first persuade and convince the above-mentioned organizations and then have them exert their influence on the company. In attempts at innovation where there is considerable resistance, this is even more crucial. But even in the "sale" of discrete services, this type of influence is important. When entering the first meeting with management, an agency staff member should have more to rely on than only his or her agency's resources or image.

Two other points about influence. An agency can frequently increase its influence in a company by coalitions with other service agencies who have relationships with the company. By combining their service packages and influence channels, agencies increase their effectiveness and multiply their influence within the company. Such a coalition of service agencies usually

reduces the interagency competition that may weaken the influence of any one agency with the company. But there are
drawbacks. The agency may find that other agencies impose
strategy limitations as a price for sharing influence. These
limitations may require revision of the service package, the
method of delivery, and the tactics used to influence the management.

Influence can only be developed when the agency has
gathered adequate information about authority, influence, and
communication channels in the company. As mentioned earlier,
identifying both the forms of influence that have worked in the
past and the key influential people in the company is essential.

Principle: Gain legitimacy by using established sponsors.

Legitimizing the agency, particularly when it is new or
innovative, may require having a more established and
influential organization, agency, or group act as a sponsor.
There are, of course, other uses to which an agency can
put a sponsor, but in terms of company development the
principal use of the sponsor is that of a "door opener."
Two points should be kept in mind:

1. Know when to advertise and when to conceal association with a sponsor. Companies differ in receptivity to a given sponsor.

2. Companies can be used in a sponsorship role. At
   times an agency can pursue job development along
   industrial lines by using influential companies who in
   turn influenced other industry members to become
   involved with the agency.

HOW SHOULD COMPANY DEVELOPMENT
RESPONSIBILITIES BE ASSIGNED?

There are two main approaches which human resource agencies have taken to planning and developing relationships with
companies. In most cases both approaches are used.

(1) Identify a small group of staff to be responsible for developing all initial company relationships. After initial contacts had been made and work agreements developed, the responsibility for maintaining the relationship should be turned over to operational staff who, until that point, may not have been involved in the agency-company relationship.

(2) Staff should be organized into operational teams. Each team might be considered a microcosmic manpower agency, representing all areas of specialization, including job development, placement, and follow-up.

The approach whereby a job development component develops company relationships and then "gives" them to operational staff is fraught with problems, and often has to do with differing views of the stake each had in the relationship. The most important among them are:

1. *Poor coordination leading to low satisfaction of client placement needs.* Developers, by the nature of their job, were usually in the field; and agency staff responsible for client placement had difficulties relaying client job needs to them.

2. *Misunderstanding by the operational staff of the agreement between company and agency developer.* Not having participated in the initial development process, operational staff responsible for implementing the agreement had difficulty understanding the actual nature and emphasis of the bargain established between the developer and the company. Promises that the initial developer had made were sometimes not known by the operational staff member and therefore could not be kept.

3. *The possibility that operational staff do not share the interest and commitment of the developer in the need for continuing the relationships on the same grounds and for the same reasons.* Company developers are usually exclusively concerned with opening company doors and getting job offerings. They are not concerned with ensuing problems, but move on to new company negotiations. Operational persons who are left to

deal with the company may have to reshape the relationship to meet their own needs in providing agency services.

Further, the developer and the operational person may bring to bear different criteria about what constitutes good companies. To a developer, a good company may be one that represents many client placements. To a placement staff member, the quality of the job, in terms of how long the client is likely to hold it and how favorable his or her chance for advancement is, may have a greater effect on whether the staffer will strive to place people into that company.

4. *Slowness of responding to company complaints about agency services.* The developer, who has already moved on to new companies, fails to see the need for working out problems that operational staff may have encountered. Expertise and influence, useful in the early stages of company development, are not brought to bear on later problems if involvement is not closely tied with the overall relationship.

STEP 2: INITIAL CONTACT

"First impressions last" is an old adage. The first rule in approaching a company is that it matters *who* you see. Different personnel in the organization have different degrees of authority and responsibility. Therefore, who you see on the first contact, as well as subsequent ones, will have varying degrees of authority to commit the company to a program.

A recurrent problem has been the failure to recognize the different levels of contact required if a service request is to be fully processed. In too many cases, the agency staff initiate a single point of contact—usually in the personnel department. They assume that all the necessary requirements would be processed by this person. They must be aware that three levels of contact are essential in situations where the agency seeks to modify some company procedure or to institutionalize a new practice.

The top executive group, the *policymakers,* of the company must be approached. The potential administrators of the program must be contacted and feasibility discussed. These administrators determine whether the program is administratively feasible in terms of the company's organizational pattern and ongoing activities and commitments. They assess the amount of company time and resources available and determine costs and the coordination needed to fulfill the program. These are questions for the management staff and a negative may terminate any further action on the request even if it has the policy maker's approval.

The *technical staff* must decide if and how the program can be *implemented*. An agency request needs more than the policy makers' stamp of legitimacy, the manager's affirmation that it is administratively feasible, and the technicians' judgment that the program can be operationalized.

One further consideration should be noted. Since the first point of contact involves policy makers and policy in the company, the agency will find it advantageous to be represented by its own policy-making executives. It is in this situation that the rules of the game are set and agency interests dictate that the agency rule makers be present. Situations where this is not done generally lead to ambiguous formulations of the agency's mandate.

"Ed Watkins of NAB has made an appointment for me to see the personnel manager" Lou tells Cathy. "That's great; see if Ed will go with you on the first visit. Also see if he can introduce you around and meet as many people as you can. It pays to know top dogs as well as line workers. Let me give you a tip: Once you meet these people, stay in contact with them. Try to get a sense of their problems and how they see our program. It is important to start with the top dogs to get the go-ahead but don't neglect people further down the totem pole."

Principle: Establish a Number of Agency-Company Contact Points

A wide number of working relationships should be established between agency and company personnel. The greater the number of working relationships, the better are the prospects for effective service delivery because: (1) more information from diverse sources is possible; (2) more people have a stake in the delivery of services; and (3) chances are greater to build a *broad* constituency that supports the program.

The agency-company relationship should involve three levels of both organizations—the policy makers, the administrators, and the operational technicians. All three levels are needed to make the program work. Multiple-service pathways are also significant in building an effective relationship. For example, where job development is combined with job placement, job coaching, and conflict mediation, the work of the job developer is apt to be more productive than in cases where job development is a single service. The interactions, contacts, and interdependence that characterize multiple-service delivery increase the receptivity for any new service.

Principle: Establish frequent, regular, and diffuse working relationships with company personnel

This is a rule of thumb. As it pertains to *initial contact,* it means that multiple linkages must be established early in the relationship. Although a single linkage is often used at the very outset of contact (for example, a job developer visiting a company for the first time), it must be augmented by other linkages immediately (the job developer informs the agency of the contact and mobilizes massive agency resources to aid in developing the company).

WHAT ARE THE CHARACTERISTICS OF THE FIRST CONTACT?

Who is the first person to contact in the company? In most agencies about one-half of the initial contacts are with upper management and one-half are with middle management. In follow-up contacts, there was a marked shift in the pattern, with three-quarters of the contacts being made with the middle management group and one-quarter with the staff of the personnel department. In other words, the initial contact should often be made at a high level and subsequent contacts shifted to lower status company employees.

Should the first contact be face to face or by phone? Often administrators and job developers make their first contacts by phone. We have noticed that many agency people have a tendency to overuse the phone and underuse face-to-face meetings in initial contacts. Phoning, while covering a wide number of companies, will usually not place you in touch with a company member who can respond to the agency request. There is also a limit to the amount of information that can be delivered over the phone.

A problem that is faced by most agency people in the initial contact is the "overprotective secretary." This is a gatekeeper role in a company and shields company executives from unwanted intrusions. The timid job developer may view a contact with such a gatekeeper as equivalent to contact with the executive, and indeed accept *her* or *his* negativism as *company* negativism. It becomes important to "psych out" the relative importance of company people in the decision-making process and to devise strategies to meet the *key* decision maker.

In the absense of an introduction by a third party, the following steps might be taken in initiating contact.

(1) Write a letter to a key executive briefly summarizing the goals of the program and past successes. Include brief printed matter to give more details. Point out how its relationship might be in the company's and the community's interest. Specify that you will call for an appointment to discuss the letter.

(2) Call the executive's secretary and ask for an appointment.

(3) Organize your presentation ahead of time. If you need a flip chart, bring it yourself. If you need access to a chalk board, ask for it well in advance. Do not ask company people to supply equipment for your presentation at the last moment.

(4) Develop a selling strategy. Why do you think company people might want the services? Would they be impressed by reviewing a contract you have made with another company?

(5) Do not try to rush a decision. Encourage company officials to discuss the program with others at the company.

(6) Provide the names of any business executives in the community who know your agency and its services. Let them know what else the agency has been or is currently involved in.

You need the following resources to follow this plan:

(1) Find out who would be the person to contact about the services (consult other agencies that have dealt with the company).

(2) Know the company in terms of information that may suggest needed services.

(3) Analyze the company in terms of information that may suggest needed services.

(4) Find out what allies that you might have in the company and use them as "character references" for the services.

WHAT ARE EFFECTIVE APPEAL STRATEGIES?

Agencies should develop a diversity of appeal strategies to meet the variety of motivations for program involvement among companies and among decision makers within a company. Gaining entry into a company will depend greatly on how the company perceives the program fitting its needs. Armed with information about the company, contact staff must remain sensitive to the needs of the company once contact has been made. They must sense what overall "pitch" is in keeping with the tone of the company and its policy and what "selling angles" should be stressed to each of the decision makers.

Generally, companies that become involved with employment and training agencies are receptive to at least one of four types of appeals which the program can provide:

(1) a source of labor supply not readily available to the company

(2) public relations benefits through involvement with the agency

(3) solving particularly troublesome company manpower problems

(4) receiving a financial incentive to offset certain personnel costs.

The agency personnel must know how to tailor the appeal to fit an individual case. Use facts about the company to structure your appeal. Ground it in the realities of the company operations. An appeal that is abstract or rests on selective interpretations by company personnel will inevitably weaken your case.

"i am not having much luck with Industrial Tire" says Lou. "I don't seem to be able to get through to them." "How are you selling the program?" "I've emphasized community responsibility and played heavily on the needs of our clients." "That may be your mistake," says Cathy, "those lines may work in some cases but not in others. Remember, a company is in business to make money and if you want to get through you have got to show them how our services can save money for them or reduce turnover. It might help if you sat down with some of their technical people and look long and hard at their production and cost problems in the light of our services."

PROTOTYPE INFORMATION FORM
FOR TARGETED COMPANIES

A.   COMPANY TO BE TARGETTED: _____

      ADDRESS: _____PHONE: _____

B.   BASIC INFORMATION

    1. Type of work performed

    _____

    _____

    _____

    2. Types of human resource surpluses and shortages found

    _____

    _____

    _____

    3. Types of jobs targetted for development

    _____

    _____

    _____

4. Previous history, if any with Human Resource Programs

_____

_____

_____

5. How many employees in geographic area

_____

6. Headquarters where Human Resource decisions are made (local, home office, etc.).

_____

_____

7. Other

_____

_____

C.   CONTACT PERSON

1. *Top Administrator (s)*   *Title*   *Phone*

   a. _____   _____   _____

   b. _____   _____   _____

   c. _____   _____   _____

2. *Others*

   a. _____   _____   _____

   b. _____   _____   _____

   c. _____   _____   _____

D.   HOW COMPANY WAS SELECTED

[ ] self-selector   [ ] planned selection   [ ] fortuitous selection

Describe process (include who key actors were)

_____

_____

_____

E. TYPES OF APPROACHES THAT MIGHT WORK WITH THIS COM-
    PANY/DEVELOPER

_____

_____

_____

F. PROBABLE SERVICE TO BE GIVEN
    [ ] expansion of company activity   EXPLAIN: _____
    [ ] modification of company activity _____
    [ ] innovations; how structured   _____

G. RELATIONSHIP OF THE TARGET COMPANY TO THE
    INDUSTRY IT REPRESENTS

_____

_____

_____

H. SOCIAL STRUCTURE

_____

_____

_____

I.   SPONSORSHIP

    1. Type of sponsorship (if any) useful in gaining access

    _____

    _____

    _____

    2. Who should initiate/manage sponsorship arrangement?

    _____

    _____

    _____

    3. Steps to be taken

    _____

    _____

    4. Other influence systems to be activated by plan

    _____

    _____

J.   STAFF PERSONS (TEAM MEMBERS) TO BE ASSIGNED
    RESPONSIBILITY OF GAINING ACCESS

Name	*Title*	*Task*
_____	_____	_____
_____	_____	_____
_____	_____	_____
_____	_____	_____

K.   TYPES OF INCENTIVES

_____

_____

_____

_____

Chapter 3

ENGAGEMENT:
The Strategy of Penetration

Access must quickly be followed by the agency increasing its penetration of the company. The two phases are usually successive, although they can overlap. Once access and entry have been established, it is important to consolidate these positions.

To do so, the agency must successfully answer important questions:

- How does the agency diagnose company problems?
- How are needed agency resources to be mobilized?
- How can an adequate information and communication system be built?
- How can an awareness of the agency's service program be created?
- How can multiple working relationships between agency and company personnel be established?

HOW DOES THE AGENCY DIAGNOSE COMPANY PROBLEMS?

The first concern is problem definition. Agency and company personnel may have different perceptions of the problem. For example, the company may view a lack of client promotion as a motivation problem while agency personnel may see it as stemming from racism. Mechanisms (seminars, interviews) must be developed to establish a dialogue between agency and company personnel. This dialogue should begin as quickly as possible. It should include a wide variety of company groups for several reasons:

(1) It identifies which groups are aware (or unaware) of the problem and the priority given to it. There may be variations of concern about the problem and it may be described in conflicting terminology.

(2) Such dialogues can be used as a device to create awareness of the problem in groups where it does not exist (e.g., among policy or operational people).

(3) Dialogues, when effective, can be a step toward involving people in the problem-solving or service delivery stage. Extending these dialogues into the service delivery stage can help determine if company personnel have changed their attitudes toward the problem or if the problem is simply being described in new jargon.

(4) The dialogues, if sequenced properly, can also be used as a feedback mechanism to keep disparate company groups in touch with what is happening.

Of course, problem diagnosis requires information. Focused interviews with representatives at each appropriate level of the company should be used to supplement the basic company data that were discussed above. The participation of supervisory and operational people is essential, but as many groups as possible should be involved and contacted by the agency.

Two other points should be noted. First, the diagnosed problem and the mechanisms for solving it should be presented in clear terms. If this is not done, the agency may find itself committed to activities which it cannot perform. Considerable care should be taken to see that selective or distorted versions are not presented and that policy makers do not have one version of the task while operational people have another. There is a need for controlled communication so that agency staff are involved in all information exchanges. A team of agency and management personnel can be entrusted with this task to insure a uniform treatment.

Second, agency personnel should allow themselves sufficient lead time before service delivery to work on problem definition. All too frequently, these activities are not planned in detail and too little time is allocated to them.

HOW ARE NEEDED AGENCY RESOURCES TO BE MOBILIZED?

Organizational penetration requires a delineation of agency resources that will be used. Thus, client counseling problems would involve the agency counseling expert, while a problem involving training would call for the services of the training expert or a curriculum designer. In some instances, the problem will be complex and a team of staff members with varied skills will be necessary. If the agency is to be a change agent and introduce innovations into the company, then it must assemble a team with expertise relevant to the assignment.

1. Should the agency have fixed teams with a mixture of people with both specialized and general skills or should staff resources be organized on an ad hoc basis to meet specific company requests? The advantages of a fixed team are several: It gives continuity to agency operations; it is easier to administer; and it gives a number of staff members the opportunity to work together for a long period of time. The disadvantage of fixed teams is the possible perpetuation of organizational units that lack the required expertise to handle an assignment. They may be assigned anyway and show poor service performance.

The other possibility is to organize teams with requisite skills when the problem becomes known in sufficient detail to identify the required expertise. The latter system is more difficult to administer, lacks continuity, and does not provide the basis for strong group identification. It is, however, the more flexible of the two.

2. The required expertise may not be available in the agency. In such cases, arrangements usually are made to either hire staff

who can perform the services or subcontract out for them. One drawback of this system is apparent in agencies where the organizational identity stresses *total* service delivery and the staff believe that they can handle all problems. There may be a tendency to provide less than acceptable service or to redefine the problem into terms that the current staff can handle. Both solutions are unfortunate and seriously impair the agency's service capabilities.

HOW CAN AN ADEQUATE INFORMATION AND COMMUNICATION SYSTEM BE BUILT?

The role of acquiring information is crucial. In many agency-company relationships, information gathering is an afterthought. Rather than being a planned activity, it becomes a salvage job. Too much information—overloading the system with random or useless information beyond the comprehension of agency staff—is as bad as too little information. Where the goals and objectives of the service activity have been clearly defined with reference to the problem, criteria for the collection of information can easily be developed. Where there is ambiguity of goals, criteria are difficult to develop and consequently service delivery and evaluation suffer.

Developing communication patterns presents parallel problems. Three organizational alternatives exist:

1. Operational teams from agency and company should remain in frequent contact, blending the formal (memos, conferences, letters, reports) with the informal (unstructured meetings, face-to-face communications). It is important that information about activities in their respective spheres of influence be shared.

2. There should be good communication links between operational people in service delivery and their top administrative superiors. Usually, the agreement for service is negotiated by executives but the performance task is passed on to operational people. The result can be a lack of continuity between the terms of the initial agreement and program performance. There

may be a need to modify the initial agreement but operational people are generally powerless to prompt changes. Good communication channels could relay their problems to executive policy makers.

3. Communication channels should operate between top administrators of company and agency. This permits an efficient exchange of important messages between organizations; gives the leaders of each some indication of how performance is being viewed among their counterparts in the other organization; and provides an avenue of communication from operational people of one organization to the top executives of the other organization. As a mechanism for resolving interorganizational disputes among operational people, it is quite effective.

HOW CAN AN AWARENESS OF THE AGENCY'S SERVICE PROGRAM BE CREATED?

One of the recurrent problems in agency-company relationships is the need to develop an awareness *at all levels of the company* of the agency's program and how it works. This awareness reduces the suspicion and resentment that are inevitable when people are confronted by the unknown. This objective is not easy to accomplish for two reasons:

1. It is difficult to reach total staff in any organization. Direct contact may be spatially impossible and questions of time and resources may restrict it. The use of the mass media (e.g., company newspapers) has some severe limitations since precise and intelligible communications may be more difficult than in face-to-face contacts.

2. Company supervisory staff may not understand the reasons for involving all subordinates in an understanding of the program. The supervisory staff may feel that the gain in understanding does not compensate for time lost on the job through contact with agency personnel. Some supervisory personnel may also deeply resent agency prerogatives in contacting subordinate staff and see it as undercutting their position as supervisors.

But, it cannot be overstressed that such awareness is necessary, particularly among company personnel who have a role in the implementation of the program and are key gatekeepers in the organization. Without it, real participation in the program on a broad base is practically impossible. The following mechanisms have proven to be effective in dealing with this problem:

(1) Hold many small group meetings, involving as many workers as possible.

(2) Educate interested company people on program content and try to spread this information by the multiplier effect. Make every effort to identify company people who have wide contacts and whose job places them in a strategic position to communicate to others.

(3) Make an agency representative available at designated time periods to answer questions of interested company personnel.

HOW CAN MULTIPLE WORKING RELATIONSHIPS BETWEEN AGENCY AND COMPANY PERSONNEL BE ESTABLISHED?

Company decisions and commitments rarely are made and implemented at one level of the organization. The decision-making process usually involves initiation at the policy-making level, organizational design at the administrative level, and implementation by technicians. A bona fide company commitment should involve participation and inputs from all three of these levels.

In working with companies to place hard-to-employ clients, agencies should establish *frequent, regular,* and *diffuse* working relationships with company personnel. These multiple working relationships should range from "firefighting" and "trouble-shooting" contacts to more regularized service contacts. As many working staff as possible, from a variety of agency units, should be in contact situations with their counterparts at all levels of the company.

Principle: Involve a Number of Agency and Company Staff in Problem Identification

The agency should involve a number of its staff in company diagnosis. Not only will a wider range of information and interpretation be gained but also this broad involvement of staff will pay off later if the same staff are engaged in working with the company.

The agency should involve as many levels of the company as possible in dialogues. A main objective here should be to get company personnel in self-diagnosis and problem solution. Supervisors and operational people almost certainly have to be present if the developed program is to be effective.

Multiple linkages are important. This statement is supported both by the conventional wisdom of practitioners and the results of research. The number of linkages established and maintained between the agency and the company varies directly with the company's placement record. In other words, you will have a higher placement rate if you have many rather than few working relationships with different kinds of company personnel.

Principle: Insist that as many of the staff as possible be involved.

Then persons should have active participation with company counterparts. There should be a greater emphasis on the necessity for agency staff to establish good working relationships with personnel at different levels and units in a company (including middle managers and front-line supervisors directly involved with placed clients).

Other factors associated with the maintenance of agency-company relations include: the way(s) in which contacts between agency and company staff are generally carried out; the degree of reciprocity in initiating these contacts; and the perceived adequacy of the contacts. Again the conventional wisdom of practitioners and researchers tells us that you can get a higher placement record if:

(1) you are involved in contacts characterized by face-to-face meetings instead of telephone contacts

(2) you have the same opportunity as your company counterpart to initiate the contact

(3) you are perceived by the company counterpart as being able to do your job, or put another way that the contact is productive.

Principle: *Agencies should stress the importance of spending a relatively high proportion of time in the field.*

This should be emphasized in procedures used for staff development and training, and reinforced during regular staff (or team) meetings. As a general principle, agency-company contacts should be carried on through some combination of face-to-face meetings and phone calls. The means of contact will situationally vary but liaison contacts involving placed clients and company personnel should most certainly be conducted in face-to-face meetings.

Finally, success in maintaining good agency-company relationships requires that:

(1) the agency's field staff have *access to employers*—that is, have the freedom and the ability to initiate contacts and negotiate with company personnel at appropriate intervals or on specific, crucial occasions

(2) company personnel have *access to agency staff members*—that the agency staff be receptive and responsive to attempts on the part of company personnel to initiate interactions with the agency.

Once entry has been achieved and a number of beginning relationships established, staff can begin the process of negotiating an operational agreement.

Chapter 4

NEGOTIATING AN AGREEMENT

There is a basic premise underlying all bargaining and negotiations between agency and company personnel: Effective communication between agency and company personnel can be translated into effective working arrangements between the organizations that they represent. The value of bargaining skills to the agency is implied in this premise. Without such skills, communications between the organizations can occur, but they may not result in the effective working relationships that are required by most agency employment and training programs.

Negotiating the working agreement is the third stage of the relationship we are concerned with. In this chapter, we will answer several important questions.

- What is the purpose of a negotiated agreement?
- What is the content of a negotiated agreement?
- How do you prepare for negotiating sessions?
- What are the steps in the negotiation process?
- How can bargaining impasses be resolved?
- How should the agreement be administered?

WHAT IS THE PURPOSE OF
NEGOTIATING AN AGREEMENT?

The negotiation of an agreement between the agency and company fulfills several important purposes:

1. The very process of negotiations involves an ongoing interchange between agency and company personnel that sharpens the goals, objectives, and interests of each party. It also airs and highlights the difficulties that must be overcome if such goals and objectives are to be achieved. From these discussions both parties probe the mutual expectations in any agency-company service program. The negotiation process is, then, both an educational and information-gathering experience for both parties.

2. The negotiation of an agreement provides an opportunity to present alternative service plans as well as to adapt a given service plan to the realities of the company situation. In one sense, the negotiation process "forces" the agency personnel to think through their program and services in greater detail and to modify them if necessary.

3. The agreement itself, particularly in written form, spells out the information, personnel, and resources that will be required for the working relationships. It is a document that specifies the *who, where, what,* and *when.* On the basis of this document, both sides can engage in some predictable planning, assignment of personnel, and allocation of resources. In the absence of such a document, there is a high degree of uncertainty and unpredictability about the content of the agency program, how it is to be delivered, and who has major responsibilities.

4. One should not overlook the fact that although the written agreement frequently has no legal standing, it does imply a certain *moral* commitment on the part both of agency and company personnel. In this sense, it can be construed by the agency as a form of "license to operate."

These observations suggest a number of reasons why a negotiated agreement is extremely important. We suggest three basic principles that should underlie the development of such an agreement.

Principle: Write, Circulate, and Review the Service Agreement

The agreement should be committed to writing. This provides not only a documented set of guidelines for service operations but such written records are stronger expressions of company commitments than "handshake agreements." Spell out who does what, where, and when.

The written agreement should be circulated widely and given exposure in the company. This reinforces the commitment made by the company.

The written agreement should be reviewed periodically both by agency and company personnel to see if revisions are necessary in view of new services offered by the agency and new operating realities within the company. A new counseling program may well strengthen existing services of the agency; changes in the labor market may create a demand for new services on the part of the company.

WHAT IS THE CONTENT OF A NEGOTIATED AGREEMENT?

The exact details of an agreement will, of course, vary from situation to situation. There are two elements, we believe, that should be present in all agreements:

(1) a "high support" component

(2) a program service arrangement component with a statement of goals, objectives, schedules, and routines that are associated with the delivery of services.

THE "HIGH SUPPORT" COMPONENT

It is not enough that an agreement specify the services to be delivered or the objectives of the service delivery. Work with hard-to-employ job applicants requires that some thought be given to supporting the job applicant in the company work environment. This usually takes the form of negotiating an agreement to remove obvious barriers to employment of the hard-to-employ, modifying the demands of the supervisory structure of the company, and giving the agency representative (e.g., the follow-up coach) certain prerogatives to advocate for his client or to intervene in crises that may occur in the company that threaten his client's continued employment.

An excellent model of a high support agreement was developed by Chicago's JOBS NOW agency in the late 1960s. It is just as valid today. Job program developers required cooperating companies to institute high support provisions for placed participants. Provisions included:

(1) lowering educational requirements

(2) the individual consideration of police records

(3) lowering minimum standards on tests

(4) assignment of a coworker as a "buddy"

(5) on-the-job consultation between participant, JOBS NOW staff, and company supervisor

(6) making contact with JOBS NOW when employee's performance faltered

(7) consultation with JOBS NOW before discharging participant

(8) providing longer periods of orientation and training.

The effectiveness of these high support agreements in promoting job retention among hard-to-employ clients is attested to by the fact that the retention proportion for companies that had instituted eight or more provisions was about three times greater than for companies that had instituted fewer than three provisions. In summary, these provisions sought: (1) to facilitate entry into the company by eliminating such barriers as testing; (2) to provide effective support for the client through a buddy system; and (3) to give the agency the right to intervene on behalf of the client in crisis situations.

Look over the access in the company form you completed at the end of Chapter 2. Think about the company you selected as

the target of your efforts. Which of the previous listed make
sense to include in your written agreement. Complete the following strategy worksheet before moving on to the rest of this
chapter.

STRATEGY WORKSHEET NO.: _____ TITLE: _____

A. Target Company: _____

B. High Support Provisions SUGGESTED	TO BE INCLUDED IN FIRST WRITTEN AGREEMENT	TO BE INCLUDED IN SUBSEQUENT AGREEMENTS
1. Lowering Educational Requirements	_____	_____
2. Individual Consideration of Police Records	_____	_____
3. Lowering Minimum Standards on Tests	_____	_____
4. Assignment of a Co-Worker as "buddy"	_____	_____
5. On the Job Consultation	_____	_____
6. Feedback on Performance, Problems	_____	_____
7. Consultation Prior to Discharge	_____	_____
8. Longer Periods of Orientation and Training	_____	_____
OTHERS THAT SHOULD BE ADDED		
9.	_____	_____
10.	_____	_____
11.	_____	_____

C. What would happen if you pushed for inclusion of the items checked for
subsequent agreements in your first written agreements?

_____

_____

_____

D. What if you were to add the items not checked in either column? To what
extent might your entire program be jeopardized?

[ ] very much   [ ] somewhat   [ ] probably not

PROGRAM SERVICE ARRANGEMENTS

A second major component of an agency-company agreement
is to specify the services to be delivered. Such agreements
require more than a mere enumeration of the techniques to be
used. They require a *detailed plan* beginning with the agency
goals and operational objectives and moving to targets for
service delivery and the schedules and routines that go hand-in-
hand with these. *Goals* are abstract statements of ends (or
future states of affairs) on which both agency and company
personnel have agreed. Goals must be broken down, however,
into a set of concrete and realizable *operational objectives.*
These may take the form "to develop a therapeutic counseling
program for new disadvantaged hires" or "to present a two-
week orientation program for new employees." The operational
objectives are less abstract than the goals and give guideline
direction for action. The operational objectives in turn must be
converted into *targets.* This is simply taking the operational
objective and assigning a time dimension to it. Thus, the operational objective to "develop a 100-man capacity job counseling
program" is converted to a target statement by giving it a
deadline—"develop a 100-man capacity job counseling program
by *September 1, 198* ." Finally, the targets must be specified in
terms of routines and specific, scheduled activities.

Principle: Develop a planned agreement with specified goals, objectives, targets, and routines.

The agency will find this a useful instrument not only to orient bargaining but also to provide and evaluate service giving.

The process can be outlined as follows:

1. Statement of Goals

specify ends to be achieved; fairly *abstract* statement but gives general purpose and meaning to agency service program

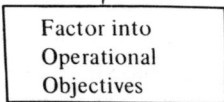

┌─────────────────┐
│ Factor into   │
│ Operational   │
│ Objectives   │
└─────────────────┘

2. Statement of Operational Objectives

specify concrete and realizable ends; fairly *specific* statement gives easily understood plan of action or procedures to achieve basic agency goal (s)

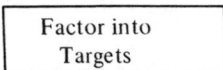

┌─────────────────┐
│ Factor into   │
│ Targets   │
└─────────────────┘

3. Statement of Targets

a statement of the operational objectives with a clear, unambiguous *time deadline* against which the objective will be actualized

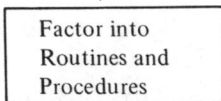

┌─────────────────┐
│ Factor into   │
│ Routines and   │
│ Procedures   │
└─────────────────┘

4. A Statement of Routines and Procedures	specific statement (s) of the *resources needed* (human and technical) and exactly *how they will be used*; special emphasis placed on time and resource commitments from agency and company; how resources will be allocated and who is responsible for what and where; must be a detailed blueprint or battle plan to actualize targets and meet abjectives and goals

Such a detailed and planned agreement has several implications. First, the agency is able to *plan* and arrange its *priorites* to combine operational staff and agency resources to service a particular company. If the detailed agreement is available, the agency administrator can assign responsibilities to staff workers with detailed work plans. Second, the agency administrator, using such an agreement, has a tool to evaluate the effectiveness of the agency operation in the company. By charting progress on each objective and observing work routines associated with that objective, the agency administrator is able to pinpoint the weak spots in a given service program as well as to identify what is required in active terms to realize a given objective.

This suggests that the agreement plan not only has implications for assessing *what is* and *what should be* happening in a given company but it also can be used as a diagnostic tool to see what routines and procedures must be strengthened, modified, or changed to make a given objective or target realizable in subsequent agency-company relationships. Finally, the agreement plan should be viewed as a device to reduce uncertainty and increase predictability on the part of management. Participation in the agency-company relationship is frequently viewed by corporate staff in terms of *costs and benefits to the company*. What time commitments must the company make? What corporate personnel must be committed? What is to be gained from participation in the relationship with the agency? These are questions that are paramount in the minds of corporate staff when approached by an agency to participate in some service program.

HOW DO YOU PREPARE FOR THE NEGOTIATION SESSIONS?

Most preparations for agency-company negotiations on the part of agency personnel should begin with a period of probing and information gathering. The negotiator's objective is to find out: (1) what services might be acceptable; (2) what services might be flatly rejected: and (3) what the company's crystallized position might finally be with respect to the variety of agency services being offered.

Negotiating an agreement requires preparation and advance planning in which: (1) it is decided who will present the agency case and be its advocate in the bargaining; (2) alternative service plans are developed; (3) the agency's position on certain issues are staked out; and (4) specific provisions of the prospective agreement are spelled out. The failure to prepare means that the agency negotiator is under heavy pressure to make snap decisions with inadequate information. The end result can be an agreement that is not geared to the problems of corporate personnel and runs the risk of not being geared to the service capacities of the agency.

SELECTING PERSONNEL TO REPRESENT THE AGENCY IN NEGOTIATIONS

The choice of personnel should be related to the objectives to be achieved through negotiations: usually (1) a policy commitment to take services; (2) specification of an acceptable service delivery package; and (3) development of a written agreement with provisions for implementation of service delivery. This may be done by an individual or a team of agency staff. The single-person approach poses a real problem, since it is rare that one individual has the prestige in the agency, knows the program operations in sufficient detail, and has all of the technical and administrative skills necessary to fulfill all of these objectives successfully.

In the selection of a negotiation team, the following considerations would seem to be important:

(1) a "top dog" of the agency should be included, with sufficient authority and prestige to interact with a "top dog" counterpart in the company. It is here that policy commitments are made and communicated.

(2) Administrative people who will be involved in administering the services (usually the heads of the appropriate service departments) should be included so as to verify the administrative feasibility of any plan that is developed.

(3) Operational and technical people who will be delivering the services should be included in order to answer the technical feasibility of any agreement that is drawn up.

It is not necessary that these persons be included in every meeting, but their combined inputs should be reflected in any negotiated agreement. A sound practice is to draw in as many of these personnel as possible in planning the negotiations to get their guidance on possible problems, specific language, and terms of the working agreement.

In addition to selecting a group to represent the agency, it is also necessary to select a spokesperson. The ideal spokesperson should:

- be articulate and persuasive
- have a detailed and realistic knowledge of agency practices, rules, and regulations
- have a knowledge of corporate practices
- enjoy negotiating and bargaining if possible.

Principle: *Make provision for a variety of expertise and diverse agency representation on the bargaining team.*

DEVELOPING ALTERNATIVE SERVICE PLANS

It is rare that a company will buy a comprehensive package of services all at once. Normally, the company will commit itself to a single service or a limited package of services. In time this commitment may be renewed or enlarged. Since there is no way to predict management needs or the specific service mix desired, it is sound practice to formulate a number of service plan alternatives beforehand. Several points should be noted in developing these alternatives.

1. The alternatives should be real choices and not merely the same plan relabelled several different ways.

2. Steps should be taken to specify and anticipate the strategy that is most appropriate in presenting each plan. It is not enough to only have different plans, sufficient thought must be given to the kinds of appeals that should go with each alternative.

3. Appropriate and frequent consultation with the agency operational people should accompany the development of each plan. This provides not only a test of the feasibility of each plan but also builds a commitment to the alternative service packages. It precludes possible intraagency conflict that may erupt because there is divided opinion on the efficacy of one plan versus another.

4. Some preliminary accounting of company attitudes and positions may be desirable to solicit information on the range of plans that would be acceptable. It is frequently possible to gain some clues by discussing the plans informally with members of the company's personnel and technical departments. By all means the plans should not be "pie in the sky" but be grounded in the realities of the company operation.

Principle: Develop alternative service plans to present to the company

The agency should see to it that it is not caught short of alternatives in presenting service plans to the company.

The company must feel that there are choices to be made—
real choices and not that it is being bludgeoned into a
restrictive course of action.

STAKING OUT THE AGENCY'S POSITION ON ISSUES

There is not much sense in taking an "all-or-nothing" stance.
You may get the nothing you bargained for. The members of
the negotiation team would do better to consider the profile
one that might make up an "acceptable deal." *The objective of
the negotiations is to get an agreement that is acceptable, not
necessarily perfect.* This requires flexibility and openness on the
agency's part.

In our experience, we have found a number of principles that
work well in most negotiations.

1. Recognize the necessity to draw in as many agency operational people as possible (e.g., coaches, counselors, and job
developers) in order to get their guidance on problems and
terms to be used in negotiating and implementing an agreement.
Since these operational people are the most knowledgeable
about agency capacities and resources, the negotiators can draw
on their "grass roots" expertise to know what to try for.
Without such knowledge, they may frequently stake out positions that the agency operational people will find difficult to
fulfill. Since operational workers must administer the agreement
and are most aware of operational problems, it is best to give
them a part in designing an agreement in which they will come
to play a significant role.

2. Review the problems and trouble spots that have occurred
in past agency-company relationships, particularly the issues
that led to disputes between agency and company personnel. Be
open and honest. If the number and mode of contact situations
have been a recurrent sore spot, the agency negotiator can
present a position on this issue designed to avoid such disputes.
An adequate review should not be confined to trouble areas but
should also identify the positions and relationships that have
worked out well in the past. This will guide the negotiator to
the positions that should be set up. We have found that it often
is sounder to begin with the positive, then to examine the
negatives. But it never pays to ignore the problem areas.

3. Review and analyze the target company's past history of doing business with agencies. Interviews with agency officials will frequently reveal what the company has been expecting elsewhere and what issues give the most trouble. This will give the negotiator some range of expectations about the company personnel.

4. Solicit from the company some statement about its future plans regarding hard-to-employ job applicants and jobholders. What objectives does the company have and what targets are under consideration? The positions that you stake out should be within the framework of these plans. Every attempt should be made to meet them halfway and gradually.

Principle: *Involve as many agency staff members as possible in developing service plans. reg. text*

The agency should see that total staff involvement is necessary in order (1) to get the largest variety of opinions and expertise in the organization and (2) to lay the basis for successful implementation by letting staff buy into the plan through participation.

SPELLING OUT PROVISIONS AND WORDING THE AGREEMENT

The specific wording of the agreement should not be an afterthought in the last steps of negotiation. The agency negotiation team must consider in the prenegotiation stages not only the *content* of the agreement but also how it is to *be worded.* The spelling out of provisions and wording of an agreement do not arise as a by-product of negotiations. In most cases they are inputs of the negotiation process. Since the language of the agreement is what operational people will have to live by, it is of the utmost importance that it be planned and worked out in considerable detail in advance of the negotiations.

- The specific language of the agreement that you propose should be thoroughly planned. Use simple terms and avoid technical terms and jargon.

- The administrators and workers in the operating divisions—the "line" men—should be consulted *before* and *after* the negotiator drafts the proposed language to see if it will work in practice.

- Consider alternative language in advance. At all costs avoid words that are ambiguous or value-laden (e.g., "evaluation" in favor of "retrieval of information").

- Anticipate what the company personnel will ask for and plan your responses. There should be no surprises if the negotiator has prepared well and knows the target company and its problems.

- In every meeting there are two agendas: (1) the proposals actually made by the company and (2) what is behind them. *Look behind every proposal and try to identify the conditions within the company that have led to this specific request or formultation.*

WHAT ARE THE STEPS IN THE NEGOTIATING PROCESS?

The conduct of negotiation is ready to begin when:

(1) the negotiating team has been selected

(2) the spokesman for the team has been picked

(3) the proposals are ready (with adequate provision for minimum, intermediate, and maximum positions).

Without some planning, negotiations can be an open-ended affair. The negotiation process should be viewed as a series of linked problem-solving meetings. Sufficient time must be spent explaining mutual concerns to both parties, developing operational objectives, diffusing potential disputes and resolving them, and working out an agreement.

These activities usually proceed through four steps: (1) establishing the negotiation range; (2) reconnoitering the range of issues; (3) narrowing the range of concerns; and (4) writing the agreement.

ESTABLISHING THE NEGOTIATION RANGE

This step is not characterized solely by hard-nosed problem solving. It begins with "getting to know each other." Considerable time may be spent on topics and issues completely unrelated to the projected service capabilities of the agency. There may be a profusion of anecdotes or personal reminiscences.

A second phase of this step involves questions by company members to learn more about the agency, its objectives, and its capabilities. The questions are usually general but some may become quite pointed. On the agency side, there is a desire to know more about the company, its problems, and its perspectives on the kind of service being offered. There are often several meetings that cover this stage.

This step may lack a clear goal orientation, but it is essential before moving on to more focused discussion. DO NOT BECOME IMPATIENT.

It is generally a good idea to give each member of both teams a chance to talk and create an identity. However, we should remember the rule about a single spokesperson. It is a recommended principle that members of the team other than the spokesman make it clear that their remarks are expansions or enlargements of the spokesperson's position rather than opposing views.

There will be a great number of questions posed by the company personnel in this step and how they are answered can determine the course of negotiations. *Questions should not be avoided* and the negotiator should not refuse to answer a question. You cannot disguise the fact that service programs frequently require time and manpower commitments from the company but exact estimates of how much time and how many personnel can be set aside for the present.

The negotiator should give himself time to think. One effective strategy is to give the ball to someone else on this team. Do not avoid issues by hiding behind the phrase "agency policy." The negotiator should be able to explain why the agency holds this position and the logic behind it.

RECONNOITERING THE RANGE OF ISSUES

While the first step was concerned with getting acquainted and establishing broad boundaries of interests, the second step is focused on conrete problem solving. Probe for commitments to certain courses of action proposed by the agency personnel. Tentative agreements occur in this step and *they should be recorded.* These tentative agreements can be easily lost in the day-to-day interactions and frequently agency and company people may be put in the position of negotiating the same issue twice. The agency negotiator talks in terms of possibilities, not certainties, in order to narrow the range of issues.

The negotiator should start with easy issues in order to record some successes at the beginning and build up momentum. Getting hung up on complicated, troublesome issues creates a climate of hostility and antagonism that could flavor subsequent steps of the negotiations. The complex issues should be put aside but not forgotten.

It is important not to oversell one service or one service plan. This step, like others, generates information. Early, rigid agreements on service delivery may be difficult to untangle later on. It is best not to engage in hard sell at this stage. Premature agreements are sometimes more dangerous than no agreements.

It is important to be realistic. The agency negotiator should know the capacities, capabilities, and resources of the agency and *limit* exploration to services that he knows can be delivered. If the service requested by the company personnel is beyond the agency's resources, this should be frankly acknowledged. This is an important point and agency personnel are frequently plied with service requests beyond the agency capabilities but fear that admission of this fact will damage the presentation of their case to the company personnel. *Do not go over your head!*

NARROWING THE RANGE OF CONCERNS

The third step of negotiations brings the features of the agreement into sharp focus. Your objective is to bridge the last gap between discussion and agreement. Timing and pacing are all important. Should the company personnel be pushed to make a commitment or should the situation be left open-ended leaving them to make the decision on their own sense of timing and pacing? Pushing for an immediate decision runs the risk to producing an agreement to which the management feels no commitment. Leaving the situation open-ended may result in procrastination and a failure of the company personnel to commit themselves at all. The choice is a hard one but the problem has to be handled.

Normally, circumstances will dictate a deadline for bargaining and reaching the point where the company personnel must make a decision. The scheduling of work within the agency and the company's scheduled expectation of a date for the services will usually impose a deadline toward which the negotiations must proceed. The agency negotiator may have to create an artificial deadline by designating a date by which discussions must conclude. This is a standard practice in most agencies because of the agency's need to service a number of companies. Unfortunately, in many cases, protracted negotiations, seemingly endless, will be necessary. Our best counsel is to fall back on your sense of humor or rely on PATIENCE, PATIENCE, AND MORE PATIENCE.

It is a good rule not to propose a final agreement until the negotiator is certain that all major issues have been discussed and all possible information is available to both parties. Avoid any temptation to phrase the alternatives in terms of yes or no. Phrase them in terms of "plan A" or "plan B." Propose alternatives and increase the range of possible solutions to the problems. The chances of agreement are slim if you present only one option.

Recognize that at all steps of the negotiations, the company personnel must check with "the man upstairs"—the superior. It is well to try to ascertain in what form or manner the presentation to the boss will be made. If possible, the agency personnel should explore the possibility of joining in that presentation to avoid questionable interpretations or to answer further questions. It would be a mistake to believe, however, that agreement with company personnel at a meeting means *company agreement.* In almost all cases, the agreement is no agreement until reviewed, discussed, and approved by top management officials.

WRITING THE AGREEMENT

The main requirement in writing the agreement is to use language that is unambiguous and can be equally understood by both parties. Jargon or technical terms are bad and can lay the basis for considerable misunderstanding. Length of the written agreement is certainly secondary to clarity of ideas, objectives, and scheduled routines associated with the services.

Two major issues should be noted in the writing of an agreement:

1. The agreement should be written as the negotiations progress and not as a final action. As agreements are reached, they should be recorded and the wording approved by both parties. The final written agreement is a cumulation of these subagreements. If the writing of the agreement is conceived as a separate act apart from negotiations, one is apt to find himself rehashing old issues and going over familiar ground. *Each subagreement should be approved as the negotiations proceed and some record of the approval distributed to both parties.*

2. Many subagreements are reached *informally* "in the back room" or in nonnegotiation situations (e.g., luncheons). Converting these informal deals into a written agreement is a major problem because they are rarely recorded on the spot nor are there apt to be witnesses to the agreement to substantiate it. A basic rule is to record everything that occurs, even in informal contact, but it is obvious that the informal contact situation frequently precludes a strong sense of agreement.

HOW CAN BARGAINING IMPASSES BE RESOLVED?

The essence of negotiating skill is to stay problem oriented. This is a basic technique for avoiding impasses. Sticking to problems avoids the charge of "drifting" or "fuzziness." But it is necessary to recognize that some impasses will develop and strategies must be learned to resolve them.

1. A basic technique is to set aside an issue that has reached an impasse and consider other issues. This results in an image of movement and momentum that would not be possible if both sides remained focused on one issue.

2. Frequently, matters may be removed from an impasse by assigning the issue to a special "study group" with representatives of both parties. This usually works with technical problems but is less useful with general issues. Thus, an impasse over the form of a reporting system may be broken through a subcommittee but subcommittees rarely settle whether an agency follow-up program should be developed.

3. In some cases, an impasse may be broken by an off-the-record conference. No notes are taken, by mutual agreement, and the information or matters discussed in such conferences are not to be made public. Speaking "off-the-record," company personnel will frequently divulge inside information that can lead to insights to resolve the impasse.

HOW SHOULD THE AGREEMENT BE ADMINISTERED?

A written agreement between company and agency is useful only insofar as it is widely diffused and understood by the personnel in both agencies. It should be a standard principle of agency personnel to follow-up the actual agreement and seek to involve themselves in the diffusion process in the company. Several methods can be used to accomplish this objective:

1. It is useful, if the management can be persuaded, to have small group meetings of company personnel at all levels (particularly those involved in the workings of the agreement) to discuss and analyze the agreement as well as to answer questions. Every attempt should be made to personalize the agreement, that is, to spell out each individual's role and stake in it. Wherever possible, the agency personnel should be on hand to provide information and answer questions. In many companies, particularly those with rigid supervisory structures, the initiation of such meetings is difficult to promote.

2. Knowledge of the agreement, its goals, and objectives should be built into company supervisory training programs. This provides a vehicle for wide diffusion of the agreement and the provisions of the agreement serve as inputs to company in-service training programs.

3. Poor administration of the agreement can undermine what was originally a good agreement. Once the agreement is signed,

the agency personnel cannot rest on their laurels; they must set up the machinery *both* to implement the agreement *and* to see if it is working. The latter point is crucial. The agreement can easily be eroded through a lack of follow-up to check if the provisions are working. It is necessary and desirable to have periodic meetings to review the agreement, involving both company and agency personnel, particularly those who are involved in implementation. In this sense, bargaining, agreement, and follow-up must be seen as part of a single process shading into maintenance of the agency-company relationship that will be discussed in some detail later.

Chapter 5

PROGRAM DEVELOPMENT:
The Strategy of Service Delivery

Program development does not end with the writing of the negotiated agreement. It builds on the foundation laid down through the negotiations process, but it continues throughout all phases of the relationships of company to agency.

- Are there some principles on which program development can be based?

- What is to be the focus of program development?

- What aspects of program development are critical to success in agency-company relations?

- Who should commit the resources needed for program development?

ARE THERE SOME GENERAL PRINCIPLES ON WHICH PROGRAM DEVELOPMENT CAN BE BASED?

We think there are. Let us explore a few. Developing a service package for a company involves at least two sets of "reference points"—client needs and company needs. Where the reference points are contradictory, some attempt may be made to compromise the program and shape it to serve both groups to some acceptable degree. The result frequently is that the program ends up only partially meeting either client or company needs.

In many cases, however, the service package is a "canned program," part of some national employment and training legislation typically involving training and post-job placement support by the agency. An agency may lack the expertise to translate the program to fit local company needs. The end result is that the program has little to do with manpower problems of a company and proves to be ineffective. The service package may be effective but the failure lies in the lack of resources and expertise needed for program translation.

There are at least two obvious advantages to having clearly defined goals in program development. First, it becomes possible to translate these goals into routines which are the backbone of program administration. Second, specific goals make evaluation of the activity more precise. But clarity and specificity of goals are not always advantages. The more specific the goals, the more restricted the opportunities to enlarge the program or to develop alternatives without changing our goals, as this may require a major renegotiation process. Loose and flexible goals make it possible to shift as experience suggests when program opportunities unfold. Involving company management in administration of service program and to needed changes can reduce company resistance to the program. It also increases the participation of others in working the bugs out of the program. Perhaps most important, it sets the stage to transfer responsibility. Since the human resource agency's services may eventually be operated by company personnel, their involvement and developing experience provides them with a foundation on which they can build.

WHAT IS TO BE THE FOCUS OF
PROGRAM DEVELOPMENT?

At the beginning it is necessary to specify whether the program's aim is to strengthen existing company practices (e.g., a successful training program), to modify a company practice, or to build some innovative practice into company operations. The first is comparatively easy; the last is comparatively difficult. When embarking on innovation, important questions must be asked:

(1) Should fundamental changes in company operations be sought immediately or is there some value in proceeding with incremental changes—a step at a time? If the latter is chosen, what should be the pace of change?

(2) Should the program restrict itself to *specific* changes of limited impact or should the program seek *general, diffuse* changes with widespread consequences?

(3) Should the proposed changes be restricted to one or two company departments?

(4) Should the program be long-term or short-term? What can be accomplished by the program in each case?

(5) Should the program be organized on a continuous basis (linking together a related series of subprograms) or should the program emphasize discontinuity (a series of discrete, unrelated subprograms)?

(6) Should the program try to involve a broad base of company people or should participants be restricted to key decision makers and technicians?

As we pointed out earlier, some agency service programs are developed piecemeal in response to specific local conditions. Others are "canned packages" that are nearly identical in all locales. These kinds of programs often fail to relate to specific company problems. A different strategy is possible—one that is commonly used in management consulting work. We call this the *linked problem approach* to program development.

This requires that the human resource agency begins by responding to management's need for solution to a specific problem. The strategy-linked problem links the solution of this problem to a series of other problems that emerge in the course of solving the first one. Let us illustrate this process. The management of Industrial Tire is concerned that they have had to discharge a number of lower skilled workers because they have had their paychecks consistently garnished. Some of these workers had originally been hired in the company by the agency. Turnover is high and company cost is excessive. One solution might be the development of a legal services unit in the company which would counsel potential garnishees and act as their advocate. The agency is willing to help but it cannot shut this program up. But in resolving this problem, the agency becomes aware that company line supervisors have negative attitudes toward unskilled, hard-to-employ workers which are factors in the problems. A special worker education program may be needed for worker and company. This may emerge as a new service activity. This has a number of advantages to worker and company. By using the "presented" problem to probe deeper, the first problem provided an opportunity to expand services to both workers and management.

Programs designed to introduce innovation generally pursue one of two leading theories of organizational change. The first presumes the need for attitude change in corporate personnel, particularly those identified as decision makers. It is assumed that changed attitudes will lead to a new outlook and this in turn leads to changes in company practices. The second theory presumes that attitude change will follow changes in practices or structure, and that these changes can be achieved directly. It is argued that changed behavior, even if involuntary, will over time result in changed attitudes. Since behavior is what we are trying to change, the argument goes, why not change it first. Proponents of this second view also argue that changed attitudes do not necessarily lead to change in organizational practices, particularly if the latter are supported by vested interests. Obviously it would be desirable to have both kinds of change, but if the agency has limited resources, one kind of change will be given priority over the other.

The selection of a change strategy is important in program development. Agency ideology and expertise frequently are factors in selection, but other factors are also operative. If the agency is psychologically inclined, it will lean toward attitude change. The theme of "friendly persuasion" through increased interpersonal sensitivity reinforces this view. Companies are also reluctant to impose behavior on their personnel and strong support is found here for giving attitude change priority.

Structural changes require both specialized expertise and the introduction of incentives or rewards. Many different kinds of influence must be used to change some property of the organization (e.g., the hiring system) that is supported by tradition or vested interests. Unfortunately, few agencies have either the expertise or the resources needed.

WHAT ASPECTS OF PROGRAM DEVELOPMENT ARE CRITICAL TO SUCCESSFUL AGENCY-COMPANY RELATIONS?

Program development is a complex of activities that amounts to much more than simply administration of a service package. In our examination of an effective agency-company relationship, we have distinguished seven clearly identifiable components of program development. Although these components shade into each other, we will discuss them as discrete items for purposes of clarification.

PLANNING AND NEGOTIATION

Although the agency has already negotiated a general agreement with the company, further planning and negotiation are necessary to translate the writer agreement into concrete actions.

Principle: *Specify Resources To Implement the Agreement*

The resources and supportive services necessary to implement the agreement previously reached with the company should be specified in considerable detail. The exact method and scheduling for the delivery of these services must be specified. This specification will involve further bargaining with the company to establish and detail resource commitments from agency and company.

This is the stage at which decisions about the operational aspects of the service program are made and remade about information that has been collected about the company, its operating procedures, its problems, and the community context in which it operates. Decisions are made on the basis of "feasibility" with the view in mind of continued and expanded agency-company relations in the future. For planning purposes, the following must be specified:

- the supportive services needed by the agency clients and company personnel to make service delivery effective
- the competencies of the company and agency staff (in order to distribute responsibility for different pieces of the service package)
- the outside resources available in the community from other agencies and companies that can be mobilized to support, enhance, or maintain the service program
- the resources available in the agency and company that can be drawn on to backstop the service program.

Selection of the supportive services should always involve *both* company personnel and agency staff. It is particularly important to involve company personnel and line supervisors who will actually be dealing with agency clients. This is not merely a matter of engineering consent. It can reduce resistance by making the rationale for the program clearer and also improve its administration—especially if the agency people have "savvy" enough to elicit suggestions from supervisors about how to adapt such services to their needs.

TRAINING COMPANY STAFF

In addition to implementing the service objectives of the agency-company agreement, the human resource agency staff may be called upon to provide training and "know-how" to company personnel in the logic, operation, and administration of the service program. The groundwork must be laid for integrating the service into "normal" operations of the company. In the long run, training company staff may be far more important than putting a particular service into practice. It creates the opportunity for agency staff to have considerable impact on company operations. Every service delivery program should be viewed as an opportunity to develop new perspectives on the part of company staff. As company personnel consolidate new perspectives and develop new skill in human resource development, it is likely that they will be more receptive to assuming responsibility for the service program.

MOBILIZING COMMUNITY RESOURCES

Program development will and should require the mobilization of a number of community resources in service delivery to the company. Local and state agencies may be approached for special services or sponsorship. Private companies may have special tools or equipment that will be needed. Some private businesses can provide supportive services to the client that neither the agency nor the company has available (e.g., consumer loans, tools). The purpose for mobilizing such community support is three-fold:

- the service program can be enriched and broadened, thus increasing prospects for effectiveness
- considerable diffusion of information about the service program occurs, laying the basis for the recruitment of "new customers"
- company personnel may be shown the opportunities and ways of securing such resources, thus laying the groundwork for the possible maintenance of the service under their auspices.

The mobilization of community resources in program development, if done in conjunction with company personnel, will set in motion new relationships between the company and community institutions. These relationships can provide the company with access to new resources.

DEVELOPING AND IMPLEMENTING "HIGH SUPPORT" PROVISIONS

Delivering the service package must go hand-in-hand with a set of provisions where the company commits itself to certain practices to facilitate the hiring and retention of clients. Getting agreement on the provisions must be followed by agency efforts to implement the provisions. The failure or inability to develop or implement these provisions can seriously undermine the soundest service program.

In the case of JOBS NOW, mentioned earlier, the establishment of the following eight provisions was related to high placement rates for agency clients:

(1) sensitizing company representatives through training to the employment difficulties and problems faced by disadvantaged workers

(2) adjustment of the company's hiring qualifications to lower levels for agency clients, as by lowering hiring requirements

(3) provision by the company of special training or orientation programs for agency clients and their supervisors

(4) expansion or upgrading of the type of jobs available to agency clients by the company

(5) acceptance and use of agency's post-placement job coaching services by the company

(6) on-the-job consultation between client, agency staff, and company supervisor

(7) contact by the company with agency staff when client's performance faltered

(8) consultation by the company with agency before discharging client.

PROVIDING AGENCY EXPERTISE ON COMPANY PROBLEMS

While the agency staff are primarily engaged in delivering specific services, staff members often bring to the company a fund of knowledge (derived from past agency experience) that can be used for general problem solving in the company. In some cases, this outside information can be used to overcome barriers related to service delivery, but in other cases it can be applied to some problem not directly related to the service being delivered. For example, knowledge of record-keeping procedures or knowing how to restructure some work operations may provide valuable information to the company.

> ### Principle: Company Use of Agency Expertise
>
> In program development, "outside information" should not be restricted to problems of immediate service delivery. The agency staff should be available as a problem-solving resource to the company. This will frequently result in higher credibility for agency staff and develop the perspective that the agency shares an interest in the problems of the total company.

PROGRAM ADMINISTRATION

A major dimension of program development is the actual administration of the services being delivered to the company. This is really an adaptation of the agency's past experience in agency-company relationships to: (1) the situational requirements of the different levels of the company and (2) the working agreement that has been established with the company.

Recognize that company personnel may have a different agenda in soliciting the service than that of agency personnel. A significant investment in program administration must be made in reconciling these diverse perspectives.

Principle: Involve Company in Service Programming

Program administration should include heavy inputs from agency *and* company personnel. Company personnel should be involved in designing the service program, in administering it, and in critiquing it periodically.

A significant aspect of program administration lies in the art of spreading or diffusing the service to other companies. If the service delivery is successful, steps should be taken to use the operations as a show piece or a "demonstration project" where the officials of other companies might view it.

TRANSLATION AND INTEGRATION OF
THE SERVICE DELIVERY EXPERIENCE

The actual delivery of the service is an intermediate rather than final step in program development. At the conclusion of service delivery, some investment must be made to translate and integrate the service experience into the regular, normal ongoing practices of the company. This objective should not be an afterthought but should be a central concern throughout the entire service delivery process.

Principle: Involve Company Management Continuously

Management should be continuously involved in the delivery process. It is particularly important to solicit their inputs in design and implementation of the program since such inputs build a company base of support, give company personnel an investment in the program, and provide the basis for a realistic adaptation of the services to the "uniqueness" of the company and to translate them into the normal practices of the company.

WHO SHOULD COMMIT THE RESOURCE NEEDS FOR PROGRAM DEVELOPMENT?

Service programs are not cheap. They involve a considerable investment of resources, personnel time and energy, facilities, units of equipment, and money, sometimes a considerable amount of political influence and prestige in the question of who commits what resources becomes a critical focus of all bargains in program development discussions. We have often heard it argued that in human resource operations it is highly desirable for the company to contribute some resources to the service program. The argument goes as follows:

- Making a resource contribution represents a *commitment* on the part of the company and is an indicator of its involvement.
- Securing resources from the company permits the agency to spread its services over a larger number of companies (i.e., a savings is possible).

- Resource contributions from the company permit an enrichment or enlargement of the agency service program.

This argument is hard to fault, but it does not address the "mix" of resources that both partners to the relationship we expected to contribute. We have found that agency-company relationships involve trade-offs between personnel and physical resources (e.g., money, space). Bargaining between the two organizations determines the mix of human and physical resources that each organization will contribute.

For an agency, money is usually a binding constraint, whereas staff time and expertise is a flexible resource that can be committed more easily. For a company, there is usually a high cost involved in contributing personnel time, particularly if these people are directly involved in the production or service process. The company would rather make a contribution of money or facilities rather than release valuable personnel from production functions. The conclusion is that a 50:50 sharing of all costs (personnel and physical) is rarely possible and even where it does occur, the program will not meet with success.

The most productive agency-company relationships are those that called for a sharing of resources, with the company usually contributing nonpersonnel resources and the agency contributing personnel. There is often resistance to committing company personnel to these service programs. We have noticed that even if such commitments are made, the personnel involved have little influence or prestige. Yet, there is a need to have key company personnel involved if the program routines are to be integrated into "normal" company operations. The agency should seek to explain this point to corporate decision makers and seek, if possible, some role in selecting company participants. Even if the agency has no voice in this decision, some company contribution of personnel is essential, even if mutually marginal to the service agreement. A total lack of company manpower in the program can impede ultimate transferability of the service program, so that some demand for manpower participation is necessary.

Chapter 6

THE MAINTENANCE OF THE RELATIONSHIP

Even the most effective agency-company relationships are not likely to endure over time without the help and guidance to mature and continue to develop. This requires that they be nurtured by both the agency and company personnel. In all too many cases, the implementation of agency-company agreements has failed because there was a lack of thought given to the maintenance of the agency-company relationship. Both the type and number of contacts that develop between agency and company personnel are key concerns. Several questions immediately come to mind:

- What are the main considerations associated with maintenance?
- Why maintain regular contact?
- What kinds of mechanisms can be set up to interchange information?

WHAT ARE THE MAIN CONSIDERATIONS ASSOCIATED WITH MAINTENANCE?

What happens to the agency's client in the company setting is a major consideration in shaping and stabilizing agency-company relationships. If there is reported failure among client referrals, this will have an impact on the agency-client relationship, regardless of whether agency personnel and company personnel develop good interpersonal relations with each other.

Thus, building good relationships between agency and company staff can be no substitute for establishing an effective follow-up service program to help the client improve his chances of succeeding in the work situation. This single fact is often lost sight of even though, from the perspectives of agency and company personnel, it is a basic building block to stabilize and expand the current service program.

Principle: Strengthen Follow-Up and Support

As a first step in maintenance, the agency should strengthen the follow-up and increase supportive services to improve the client's chance of making a "good showing" after placement. The best advertisement for the program is a successful job placement.

Serving the client, as well as the company, does not end with placement. Retaining the job—and the difficulties associated with it—may require a greater measure of resource investment than the placement process itself. The follow-up should not be merely nose-counting but rather an honest effort to back up the client with the resources that he needs to succeed.

Having made our point, it is now time to make some commentary on other important considerations.

OTHER CONSIDERATIONS

REGULAR CONTACT PATTERNS BETWEEN AGENCY AND COMPANY

Just as regular contact with company personnel was a prerequisite for success in the access stage, so regular contact is important in the maintenance stage. Regularity of contact performs three important functions in maintenance: (1) it establishes the service given and the service giving as a normal part of the work environment rather than as episodic, intermittent, and haphazard events; (2) it lays the basis for a relationship associated with stability rather than crisis (showing up only when the client or the relationship is in trouble is a poor basis for regularizing the relationship); and (3) it provides agency staff with a continuous flow of information that can be the basis for adjusting the program to new realities.

COORDINATION AND COMMUNICATION MECHANISMS TO PROVIDE EASY INTERCHANGE OF INFORMATION

The coordination of activities and communication between company and agency personnel is not automatic; it must be provided for. Coordination of activities has its roots in the program development stage where a division of labor is worked out between agency and company personnel, where authority and responsibility is spelled out, and where routines and schedules are established. Thus, coordination as an activity is the working out of plans developed earlier.

Coordination may be based in a joint committee, or in a commonly agreed-upon member of the agency or company, or in an outside contractor who does not belong to either organization. Whatever the mode, there is a clear need to establish a mechanism of coordination that both sides respect and can live with. In a similar manner, there must be provision for a communication mechanism. There may be a range of mechanisms: some planned and some unplanned.

There may be regularly scheduled meetings where a wide variety of information is exchanged. There could be regular exchanges of organizational memos or policy statements. There could be written summaries of agency and company activities supplied to both sides. Another possibility, not to be overlooked, is the flow of information that passes between organizations through casual, unplanned contacts—another argument for frequent, although informal, contacts between personnel from both organizations.

FOLLOW-UP PROCEDURES TO CHART CLIENT
PERFORMANCE AND GIVE SUPPORTIVE SERVICES

We have already discussed the need to follow up the placed client with services. Specific needs of the hard-to-employ in a work place cannot be met by company personnel because they lack the expertise or training to identify the needs or to service them. The follow-up of the placed client is not only supportive to the client but it is supportive to company personnel as well.

In the process of serving the client, agency personnel show company staff how to deal with a wide range of client problems and in effect begin the process to transferring the expertise to the company staff. In this context, the supportive services both aid to stabilize the client and to give new perspectives and expertise to the company personnel.

FOLLOW–UP PROCEDURES CARRIED OUT ON A
REGULAR BASIS TO EXAMINE THE RELATIONSHIPS
BETWEEN COMPANY AND AGENCY

The agency-company relationship negotiated in stage 3 is not immutable and is subject to change because circumstances change. The company may develop new policy directions; the agency may have new services available; both organizations may acquire new personnel; or the labor market may change. Any of these circumstances may cause a disruption or modification in the relationship. For this reason, the relationship should be under continuous review by both parties. Four questions are basis to such a review:

(1) What new initiatives and programs can be developed jointly by the organizations to expand the services to older clients or to include new clients?

(2) What were the original goals and expectations of both parties in the relationship and have they been met or frustrated?

(3) What recurrent or unique problems surface in the relationship and what options are available to cure them?

(4) What has transpired in the program in activity terms since the program began?

Such views should be continuous and involve staffs of both organizations. Provision should be made for involvement in the review on a regular basis of the "top dogs" of both organizations, for example, quarterly. The important element is to provide an occasion where top, middle, and lower level staff of the agency and the company can see what has transpired, what is transpiring, and what will transpire in the future.

DISPUTE-HANDLING MACHINERY TO HANDLE PROBLEMS THAT DEVELOP IN THE RELATIONSHIP

Disagreements and disputes can be expected in any relationship. Some problems can be handled ad hoc but it is best to develop means of handling the sticky problems. Who should be involved in handling client-company disputes? How should agency involvement be integrated with the company's normal and regular grievance procedures?

We have three suggestions:

(1) involve company staff that has the authority to handle the problem and the same is true of agency staff

(2) agree on what problems should involve the top dogs of the organizations, do not involve them needlessly

(3) be sure that the problem solving involves an implementation plan so that recommendations can be translated into concrete actions.

The maintenance stage is an extension of the process of solidifying the program in terms of stabilizing and regularizing it. It is an important stage because all of the promises and strategies of earlier stages must now be normalized and set into concrete.

WHY MAINTAIN REGULAR CONTACT?

In effect, we have already answered this question. Our observations of practice in a number of settings suggests that:

- The greater the number of contacts between agency and company, the more successful the client's experience in the company is likely to be.

- The fewer the contacts, the less successful.

Examples of regular and ongoing contacts include the following:

(1) regular visits to personnel department and supervisor to check progress of placed clients

(2) visits to review progress of the service program in terms of goals set earlier

(3) visits to top dogs to review and sell new agency services

(4) visits to check out changes in production system and possible needs for new workers

(5) visits with personnel department to review job descriptions and qualifications

(6) visits to gatekeepers (informed friends) to check on receptivity of service program.

Principle: Establish and Maintain Multiple Relationships

Employment and training agencies should place considerable emphasis on establishing and maintaining multiple working relationships with companies accepting their clients as referrals for jobs, especially with companies having above average records for placing agency clients.

The application of this principle will ordinarily call for more widespread involvement and active participation among agency staff in agency-company relations. In addition to staff members, particularly job developers, having ongoing dealings with companies, other agency staff in other roles and/or units should function as "linkage agents." For example, the agency administrator, counselors, and coaches should interact with company staff from time to time.

Agency personnel who are traditionally desk-bound might profit considerably from such contacts. The agency counselor might find that such contacts give him or her a more realistic picture of the world of work while the counselor's company counterpart might gain a greater knowledge of client problems and needs from an agency member who is more knowledgeable on this matter.

Principle: Involve a Cross-Section of Agency Staff

The agency should develop contact systems which directly involve the *agency* staff who are spread over different units or departments. This means creating more widespread involvement and active participation among agency staff in agency-company relations. It also means that in addition to staff having ongoing dealings with companies, other agency personnel in other units or roles should be called on periodically to act as linkage agents with company managers at various levels as well as front-line supervisors, if possible.

Principle: Frequent and Regular Contacts With Companies

Agencies should contact companies frequently and regularly. More frequent and regular agency-company contacts are associated positively with high client placement, while less frequent and irregular contacts are associated with low client placement. The exact number of contacts which agency staff should make with a company depends on a number of concerns, but agencies should generally assume that the number is higher than they usually believe necessary or possible. Monthly contact is not an unreasonable goal.

Companies with higher placement records (more successful employment of the hard-to-employ) usually initiate more contacts with agency personnel more than companies with lower placement records. This requires that agency people be open and receptive to company-initiated contacts, even when such contacts are initiated to deal with uncomfortable or unpleasant problems. Promoting these kinds of contact can enhance and expand the relationship. An important sign of an effective company-agency relationship is when company personnel contact the agency rather than waiting for the agency to contact them.

WHAT KINDS OF MECHANISMS CAN BE SET UP TO EASE INTERCHANGE OF INFORMATION?

Job developers (or whatever the agency calls its main employer-contactor) should spend a relatively high proportion of his or her time in the field. As a general principle, agency-company contacts should be carried on through some combination of both face-to-face meetings and phone calls. The optimal combination will, no doubt, vary according to the "situational requirements" for relating to each particular company. However, the more important kinds of interactions (e.g., acting as liaison between placed clients and company staff) should, most certainly, be conducted via *face-to-face meetings.*

Agency staff working most directly with companies as job developers should each have ongoing contacts with at least three different company officials. Given the turnover in most large companies, the development of a working relationship with one individual may be fragile since his or her leaving may jeopardize contact with the company.

An important way to establish numerous linkages quickly is to arrange agency-company *group* meetings early in contact procedures. In this way, a number of agency people meet a number of company people. Individual follow-up contacts should be made soon after the meeting to deepen the personal relationships. Some degree of informality should be injected into these one-to-one associations.

This approach increases agency-company contacts geometrically and rapidly creates a contact *system.* It permits the agency's employer contactors to begin moving around the company and keeping their eyes open for involvement. Success in maintaining good agency-company relationships requires that the agency's field staff have ready access to *employers*—that is, have the freedom and the ability to initiate contacts and negotiate with company personnel at appropriate intervals or on specific, crucial occasions.

Agency employment staff often feel self-conscious and insecure about demands of time and attention they are making on company personnel. They feel that if they seek the involvement of "too many" company officials, the company's tolerance point will be reached and the relationship will be soured. That operational reality exists; some company personnel will be somewhat disturbed by being asked to become involved with the agency. Because of their insecurity when reporting to the agency, some contact staff negatively exaggerate the company's feelings. Agency administrators must deal productively with staff feelings, but they should not be intimidated by those feelings, nor should they ever sacrifice the need to require staff to involve many different people in agency-company efforts. Agencies generally should strive to surpass what individual agency staff feel to be a company's tolerance level.

It stands to reason that the frequency and diversity of contact situations will be related to the make-up of the agency service package. A "single-service" package will only involve one or two company people, and at best, infrequently. This suggests that from the beginning, the agency staff should try to develop a "comprehensive package" of services that means almost automatic involvement of different company departments. A team approach is helpful in spreading involvement over various agency units and in developing multiple contacts with the company. The more specialties represented on the team, the more likely that it will be possible to establish contact with different specialists in the company.

Principle: Establish and Maintain Ongoing Visitation

The agency should establish and maintain a regular pattern of ongoing visitations, supplemented by visits to deal with matters requiring immediate attention. The prime application of this principle should focus on the relationship between agency staff (particularly coaches) and front-line supervisors of agency clients.

Principle: Keep Scheduled Visits

The agency staff should keep scheduled visits whether or not the company or its placed clients are having problems. Lack of regular visitation may impede the necessary routine of reporting problems and sharing information between agency and company personnel. If the coach is slow in getting to the supervisor, the problem which was serious at the time, and which may still be potentially explosive, often appears to diminish in importance.

Principle: Use Visits for Intelligence Gathering

The agency should use frequent visits as an educational and "intelligence" tool. Company and agency staff should decide once and early on a regular schedule of frequent visitations. This is recommended over establishing different schedules periodically. All schedules have to allow for emergencies. Missing appointments of course harm the relationship. Always going to them prepared generates a sense of seriousness and determination which should always be maintained.

Frequent visits to the company help agency staff learn more about the company, its organizational make-up, its employee benefits and programs, and its special and individual "atmosphere." Since part of the agency's task is to match candidates with jobs that have potential, frequent visits result in a more realistic picture of what the company can offer to the client.

Also, frequent visits allow agency staff to gain information which will be useful to the agency, particularly in increasing the scope of involvement as well as in enhancing the quality of service.

By keeping to the schedule of visits whether or not the company or clients seem to be having problems, coaches and job developers will strengthen both the agency-company and client-company relationships. Both relationships are based on some form of understood guarantee that even if agency staff are not working on solving problems at any one time, they are always ready and available to deal with problems. Constant contact is a tangible demonstration and reminder of that basic guarantee.

Chapter 7

ASSESSMENT AND EVALUATION
OF THE RELATIONSHIP

The next step in the process is to evaluate the agency-company relationship. This activity is not time-bound but is continuous during the seven-stage process. You must ask yourself: Has the relationship been worthwhile and has it met the expectations both of the agency and company personnel? Has the relationship been a good investment when compared with those investments that might have been made in other companies?

In order to answer these questions, three preliminary questions must be asked:

(1) What criteria and perspectives shall be used to evaluate the relationship?

(2) What information must be gathered to assess the relationship?

(3) What should be done with the evaluative information?

WHAT CRITERIA AND PERSPECTIVES
SHOULD BE USED FOR EVALUATION?

Evaluating the effectiveness of agency-company relationships is a difficult task. The criteria that should be used to determine whether an agency is fulfilling its mandate must first be developed. Clearly, an initial reference point is the agency's goals. Goal definition, however, is more complex than it may appear. An agency has multiple constituencies which must be considered and each of them may have a very different idea of what the agency's goals should be. These constituencies include the agency's funding source, its staff (both administrative and line), its clientele (both hard-to-employ and company), its community, and its network of relationships with other agencies. These groups may view agency-company relationships from very different vantage points and therefore have varying expectations regarding outcomes of agency activities and standards of effectiveness.

How, then, do agencies judge the relative success and effectiveness of their activities with companies? We have found that agencies tend to define effectiveness in four ways. These categories are not mutually exclusive since agencies usually use more than one criterion.

ATTITUDE CHANGE

Some agency workers believe success has been attained if individuals have improved the ways they relate to one another. This is particularly true of attitudes about race and the disadvantaged worker. Some agency workers believe that the extent to which they have informed company personnel of the problems encountered by disadvantaged workers determines a successful outcome. Clearly, one pitfall is the difficulty of measuring whether a change has occurred and if so, how long it will last. Those agencies which place heavy emphasis on human relations training for company personnel are most likely to use attitude change as an index of success. Attitudinal change in and of itself does not mean behavioral change and a frequent pitfall is equating achievement of attitude change with changes in behavior that are more apparent than real.

POLICY CHANGE

Here effectiveness is determined by evidence of alterations in company policy which favorably affect the hard-to-employ. In essence, this category of criteria consists of statements, either verbal or written, of a company's intention to make operational changes. The important distinction here is that such statements are intentions, not commitments; job pledges, not slots.

OPERATIONAL CHANGE

Many agencies evaluate goal achievement or the basis of policy changes in the company. The company may have altered its entry level requirements or have begun to screen in, rather than screen out, workers. It may have opened pathways of upward mobility for the disadvantaged, made training opportunities available, reduced rates of turnover and absenteeism, or provided supportive services to assure better retention. Success is measured in terms of functional changes that directly affect a company's hard-to-employ workers. Operational changes are more visible and hence more easily measured than either attitude or policy changes. Although more concrete evidence of change is available, agencies cannot be sure *they* are responsible for changes in company functioning.

CHANGE IN ORGANIZATIONAL PERSPECTIVE

It is not clear whether there is a causal relationship between the impact of operational changes and the development of a more enlightened and progressive organizational perspective. The essence of this criterion is evidence of an ongoing commitment to the disadvantaged—an institutionalization of operational change. This is the only standard that includes a time dimension as a measure.

When agency workers do not have any standards by which they can judge the success of their work, they may believe that each company contact is so idiosyncratic that no across-the-board criteria can be developed. Obviously, the evaluation of agency work with companies is not easy, nor is gaining assent on whether the agency has been successful. Consequently, staff may never be completely certain what their effectiveness, if any, has been. In this context, the agency may fall back into simple and specific activities (e.g., filling job orders) that can be evaluated with more precision. In the end, the agency may stop innovative activities altogether. Agency personnel use three approaches to these evaluation criteria.

The "mushy approach" is characterized by agency personnel who report that "things must be going well because the company is continuing the service arrangement with the agency." Continued acceptance of the service by the company is regarded as an indication that the agency program is "successful." A company may continue to take services for reasons other than gains from the service program (e.g., political or public relations motives). Mere acceptance of the service does not tell you whether the operational objectives are being achieved.

In the *"gut feeling approach"* agency personnel report that "in their judgment the agency-company relationship is a success." The reason for this judgment varies and differs from individual to individual. It is frequently based on personalized, individualized experiences and may reflect the goals of the individual worker rather than the operational objectives of the agency. Since judgments differ among individual workers, there will be a number of judgments, many of them contradictory. The end result is that the outcome of the relationship will remain in doubt because consensus on success or failure will rarely be achieved. A third, and "harder" approach is possible.

"Hard approaches" require that the evaluator collects information from company personnel records on actual placement and retention of agency clients (the payroll register gives objective data on these variables and the data are free of the perceptions or judgments of individual respondents). This approach is linked to the operational objectives of the agency as written in the negotiated agreement and thus reflects the relative success that has been achieved in reaching these objectives.

Perhaps the perspectives used in evaluation are even more important. In comparing effectiveness of the agency service package across many companies, a double set of perspectives is often found.

The first centers on the extent to which a set of *operating conditions* has been achieved between agency and company personnel (e.g., the degree of rapport, the degree of congruent perspectives, or the degree of acceptance by the company of a high support agreement). The achievement of these operating conditions is important and vital to any effective work with the company.

The second centers on *outcomes* (i.e., *what,* if anything, has been achieved, or changed, given the agency-company relationship). These outcomes are *dependent on* but *not the same* as operating conditions.

In many evaluations, the two perspectives become confused. Establishing a set of ideal operating conditions does not necessarily mean that the agency personnel have been effective with that company. Even from ideal operating conditions, there may be few tangible outcomes related to the established goals of the agency. Establishing ideal operating conditions is a prerequisite for effective outcomes but should not be viewed (in terms of evaluation) as an outcome in and of itself.

In evaluating agency-company relationships, consider the following two principles.

Principle: *The agency-company relationship should be seen in a time perspective involving different success measures at different points in the relationship. Develop different success measures for each time period of the relationship.*

At the early stage, consider the:

- number of contacts established with top dogs of company
- number and regularity of meetings with administrative and technical personnel in the company
- verbal or written statements of policy change
- alterations of personnel practices
- improved perspective on disadvantaged workers
- negotiation of an agreement in progress.

At the middle stage, examine the:

- signing of a negotiated agreement

- significant company involvement in agency service programs (e.g., numbers of employees, frequency of service)
- strategic planning to regularize services
- substantial time commitment of company staff to service program.

At the late stage, determine the:

- significant increase in job openings for agency clients
- significant increase in placement rate for agency clients
- agency training and service programs incorporated into regular company operations
- company request for more services to a wider employee population.

What is important here is to arrange criteria in some sensible temporal order and not make the error of using late stage criteria at some early point in the relationship. Do not expect too much too soon.

> *Principle: Use different measures and techniques to assess success of the relationship.*

Use more than one measure to index success criteria. Thus, "client adjustment" may be measured by job placement rates, retention rates, quality of the job, opportunity for advancement, and job satisfaction. You are on safer ground using a range of variables to make up your success measure rather than using one indicator.

Use more than one technique to produce the information that you need to measure success. Combine data from surveys, records, and observations as a basis for judgment. This strengthens the basis of your success measure. Be precise in your observations and keep detailed notes on the observations, how and why you made them. Remember that your evaluation should be available for checking by someone else.

WHAT INFORMATION MUST BE GATHERED
TO ASSESS THE RELATIONSHIP?

Gathering information is an essential activity in any evaluation. The type of information required is dictated by the evaluative questions being posed. Six basic questions should be answered in an evaluation in order to reduce reliance on "gut level" or "mushy" approaches. Each requires different information.

1. Is the agency staff expending enough effort in this company?

Information required: number of company contacts made; number of hours spent in the field; number of trips made to the company; number of meetings with company officials; number of meetings with company administrative and technical staff.

2. How effective has the staff been in achieving goals set in the negotiated agreement?

Information required: number of actual job placements compared to the target set; number of services delivered compared to the target set.

3. What has been the impact of the service program at this company on our caseload of clients?

Information required: increase or reduction in caseload; number of new client applications; increase or decrease in client population to be served.

4. What has been the cost of the program at this company compared to other companies?

Information required: per capita client service cost and average cost of staff effort compared to data at other companies.

5. Is there a favorable cost-benefit ratio at this company?

Information required: staff costs compared to value of job openings (in numbers, quality and dollar value); staff costs compared to value of potential client earnings.

6. Have we satisfactorily solved all of the problems that we have encountered in this company?

Information required: documentation of problems encountered, options considered, and successful solutions; detailed accounts of interactions between agency and company staff; detailed record of innovative practices.

The questions to be posed, and the information to be sought, depend on the evaluative style of the agency and agency familiarity with different evaluative modes. There is no rule that says that more than one of these questions can be asked in any given evaluation. Cost and resources may indeed be the ultimate determinant of which questions are posed and what information is sought.

WHAT SHOULD BE DONE WITH EVALUATIVE INFORMATION?

Perhaps more than in any other human service activity, evaluative information on agency-company relations must be put to work and utilized during the different stages of the relationship. We see five different uses to which the information could and should be put to use.

(1) identify problems for solution by joint action

(2) identify what strategies are working and which are not

(3) identify successes and failures in client job placement

(4) provide feedback on program progress to agency and company personnel

(5) identify new service initiatives that could and should be undertaken.

Evaluative information should be fed back on a continuous basis and at regularly scheduled meetings. Scheduling these regular feedback sessions should be initiated very early in the relationship.

Since this negotiated agreement is a working standard for actions, some of the evaluative data must be used to ascertain whether the provisions of the agreement have been implemented. It is this information that sets the scene for the final stage of deciding whether the agency should continue working with the company or to disengage. We turn to this issue in the concluding chapter.

Chapter 8

DISENGAGEMENT:
The Strategy of Withdrawal

The last stage of the relationship involves the decision to disengage the agency from the company—or, in the language of human resource developers, "whether to close the company out, put it in mothballs, or continue to work it." The termination of an agency-company relationship may occur in any stage from "access" to "evaluation and assessment." In many cases, the company contracts for a single service and there is the assumption that the agency personnel will leave on the completion of the assignment. At other times, both sides assume the relationship is open-ended and has no terminal date (e.g., in job placement or job development programs). There may be an implied agreement that either side could terminate the relationship at any time. We must also consider that there can be a *forced withdrawal* coming in the aftermath of some dispute or the company decision that "it has had enough."

A number of questions can be asked about disengagement:

- When is withdrawal necessary?
- Who should make the decision to withdraw?
- What are effective principles for disengagement?

WHEN IS WITHDRAWAL NECESSARY?

Agency personnel will, under certain conditions, be faced with the decision about whether and when to withdraw from the company. This decision can be made within the context of:

- goals and objectives negotiated in the written agreement in the third stage have been substantially achieved

- competing service opportunities in other companies (i.e., "where can we do the most good?")

- evaluating the effectiveness of the relationship ("what have we accomplished here?")

- allocating staff and resources in relationship to achievements ("how much is it costing us to stay here?")

- assessing the impact of the relationship on agency clients ("what have we done and what has the company done for our placement here?").

Making the decision to withdraw requires knowing when the time is ripe. It requires withdrawal and disengagement between the entire range of individuals in the agency and the company that have consolidated the relationship between the two organizations. Disengagement should not be a hasty decision. Consider the following questions:

(1) Is it necessary to terminate service contacts with the company or can the relationship be renegotiated?

(2) If withdrawal is decided upon, what contacts and communication arrangements with company personnel may persist?

(3) Can withdrawal be sidetracked in favor of new service arrangements?

(4) If withdrawal is decided upon, what "agency presence" can be left behind (i.e., is some arrangement possible by which the agency services in the company can become a "normal" part of company operations, run by company personnel)?

It is never necessary to think only about a *total* withdrawal. Renegotiating the relationship and agreements should always be considered a viable option. You should consider not only why the current service package is not working but also how to replace it with viable alternatives. If withdrawal is deemed necessary, the essential point is to provide for the continuity of the services whether on a limited basis by the agency or whether administered and delivered by company personnel. It is necessary to leave a service residue in place. A long-term goal from the beginning is to start transferring the service delivery function to company staff so that agency withdrawal will not disrupt the services program.

> *Principle: Disengagement should not mean complete termination of the service package.*

The issue is frequently not whether withdrawal should take place but what underlying network of motives and relationships has raised the question of withdrawal. A series of steps must be taken by the agency administrator to ascertain the dynamics that underlie the issue of withdrawal.

(1) Question *all agency personnel* who have any contact with the company. Do not confine yourself only to the agency member who strongly urges withdrawal. Solicit all opinion on what has been accomplished in the company and what could be accomplished.

(2) Question *key company personnel* that are involved in the agency-company relationship. Solicit all opinions on the strengths and weaknesses of the relationship, as well as what has been accomplished and what could be accomplished.

(3) Solicit from both groups information on *how the relationship could be restructured* to open new service possibilities, particularly what personnel, technologies, and strategies could be tried. Just because the old relationship is in trouble, this does not mean that new relationships are not possible. Your analysis of the old relationship should be done in the context of what *new* relationship is possible.

(4) Gather a *full package of information* on the history of the relationship, not bits of information. You should want to

know not only about the interpersonal relations between agency and company personnel but also ask:

- How have the clients fared at this company?
- What disputes have occurred and how have they been handled?
- What has been the pattern of sponsorship of agency services among corporate decision makers?
- Are there delegate agencies or community organizations that are tied in with the agency service program in the company? Would withdrawal hurt their relationship with the company?

Principle: *Ascertain the negatives and the positives of the relationship*

Withdrawal should not be a question of "whether to go or to stay." It is a *net effects issue* where you have to balance the pluses and minuses of *all* agency operations at the company. The interpersonal relations between agency and company staff may be poor but client placements may be effective. The question then becomes: Can I sustain or remedy these personal relationship problems when the payoff is high for the clients?

You should not overlook the fact that the decision to disengage may be initiated by the company and may have nothing to do with a relationship crisis. The company may indeed want to terminate the relationship because it has succeeded in that:

- the company now has the willingness and capacity to go it alone
- the company is willing to commit resources to regularize and normalize the services as part of its own operations
- the company has expanded its own services to include agency services.

These outcomes are desirable but you should examine them for new service possibilities from the agency. The disengagement in these instances is a positive rather than a negative happening.

WHO MAKES THE DECISION TO WITHDRAW?

Disengagement decisions are poorly made when:

- there is no clear measure of whether the agency-company relationship was effective or ineffective
- there was no logic for balancing successes and failures in a wide range of agency services
- there was no clear indication of who was to make the decision to withdraw.

> *Principle:*   *The administrator should involve a wide range of staff in the withdrawal decision.*

These tasks are best performed by the agency administrators for a number of reasons. Agency administrators are the only agency people with sufficient clout to draw together the variety of information required in the decision. They are in central roles enabling them to solicit information from the widest range of agency and company personnel about the nature of problems and how to resolve them. In contrast to other agency personnel, they have access to centers of corporate decision making where the question of withdrawal may finally have to be brought.

In contrast to operational people on the firing line, they are at a distance and view the relationship more objectively. Often they know the community and have a sense of the "hidden agenda" that has led some of the key actors to promote withdrawal.

Although the final decision belongs to the agency administrator, he should not forget that staff people have both vested and emotional interests in the relationship and insights into how it might be restructured. He should involve them in the decision as

more than mere information suppliers. Communicating the decision to withdraw should be a face-to-face situation, followed by
a letter that specifies the decision and what options are open for
continuing some form of the relationship.

WHAT ARE THE PRINCIPLES OF DISENGAGEMENT?

Disengagement is a sensitive activity and affects the personnel
from both organizations. It must be handled with tact and
considerable planning.

A *forced* withdrawal from an agency-company relationship
usually involves a crisis where the paramount question for the
agency is: "What can be salvaged?" By way of contrast, the
voluntary disengagement process involves a planned, purposive
set of actions that are the natural culmination of an agency-
company relationship. The question for the agency is: "What
can be left behind?" The goal is to cement and support the
outcomes that have been achieved at every stage of the relationship.

Principle: Leave a presence in the company

In withdrawal, the agency should leave a "presence in
the company." This could involve training company staff
to take over when agency personnel continue to work with
the company on some unofficial arrangement. Arranging
for new additions to company staff to give the service is
one answer. Permitting agency staff to take jobs with the
company is another.

The outcomes that have been achieved as a result of the
relationship (e.g., new job coaching procedures or new personnel practices) will not maintain themselves automatically.
The company personnel must be worked with to build for the
future support and maintenance of these innovations after the
agency personnel have departed and are no longer associated
with them.

The disengagement process should be structured around five basic sets of activities.

1. The disengagement process should be *planned.* It should not be an afterthought or come at the *end* of the relationship. The disengagement process should be broken down into a series of objectives at each stage of the relationship and steps taken to meet these objectives.

2. The agency personnel must attempt to leave *residues* of the agency operations in the company. For example, an agency-developed training program (or important elements of it) should be integrated into normal company operations. This will require joint planning between agency and company personnel as well as the development of alternative resources to maintain the outcomes of the program.

3. Before leaving, agency personnel should examine what has been accomplished at *each level of the company* and seek to keep these achievements continuing. For example, as a result of agency operations, there may now be:

- a periodic review of minority group employment patterns by the policy makers
- regular meetings of administrators to discuss service options
- new practices among operational workers to support the employment of minority group members.

The departing agency personnel must give some attention to continuing the activities on all three levels of the company. What may be necessary and desirable is a series of *exit interviews* with all of these groups, jointly analyzing and planning how gains may be sustained. The agency personnel must also be aware that some minimal agency contact may be necessary for some time to come if these gains are to be preserved.

4. The last step in disengagement should be to return to the corporate decision makers the responsibility for program maintenance. The successes and/or failures of the service program must be articulated as well as the formulas for sustaining the gains. It is in this group that the decision for maintaining gains must be made. Make the case for maintaining outcomes. Do not

rely wholly on the subordinate company personnel to make the case for maintaining outcomes. In each organization, information is selectively filtered upward and the "top dogs" in the company can be given a less than accurate picture of outcomes and resources necessary to sustain them. The exit interview with the corporate decision makers is *important* and *must* be planned. Ideally, it will unfold the total story of the agency-company relationship and what options are now open to the company to further the gains from the agency-company relationship.

5. Disengagement frequently occurs at the point of diminishing returns. The agency has achieved *most* of what it set out to achieve and further gains have not been forthcoming, or have been marginal. At this point a *streamlining* of the program may be *both* necessary and desirable. Old service packages may have to be replaced by new service options. The total program may have to be "pruned" to adapt it to the realities of company operations. In these contexts, *some* disengagement is necessary to make the program more workable.

Continuous monitoring of the agency service delivery and what it is achieving in the company is necessary. The service delivery process must be related to a series of objectives for each stage of the program. The "scorecard" should indicate achievements as well as failures in order that some "streamlining" can occur at any point in the agency-company relationship. Emphasis must be placed on changing the service product line to fit new company needs or to "cut losses" on services that have proved to be unworkable.

Through our discussion we may have seemed to repeat some of the working principles time and again. A number of them appear in several chapters. The reason for our emphasis and re-emphasis are rather straightforward. Some of the principles can be equally applied to each one of the seven stages and thus are general principles underlying the total process. For example, agency people at all levels of the organization should make inputs into the decisional process at all stages. This very involvement of staff performs several positive functions in all stages of the relationship—increases the range of information gathering; provides for staff motivation to participate in implementation; and builds loyalty and commitment to the program.

These are all gains for the agency management but at the same time they pose risks. The agency administrators may favor this mode of operation but it may inescapably clash with the management authority style of the company. This may be the ultimate problem: The two organizations are different in administrative style, ideology, goals, staff, and expertise. Built into these differences are bound to be bases for conflict. The anomaly is that these two organizations must build cooperative working relationships against this background of differences.

Consequently, the agency may have to modify or alter some of the principles in this guide to make them fit the realities of relationships with companies. The principles in this guide should then be regarded as broad guidelines for action rather than rifle-shot prescriptions.

We think the challenge of building effective agency-company relationships is a great one. It takes courage, imagination, and perserverance when things seem to go badly. It takes consistency when things seem to fit too neatly in place. It is a challenge we know you are up to. Our clients, after all, are the prime beneficiaries and that is what human resource development is all about.

APPENDIX
Practice Principles in Establishing
Agency-Company Relationships

The information contained in this Appendix is closely linked to the material developed in Chapters 2 through 8 above. In these chapters, we discussed agency-company relationships from the perspective of a *system* of actions and prescriptions that must characterize the agency as a total entity. In this Appendix we focus on the two roles in the agency that are critical to agency-company relationships: the administrator and the job developer. For each one of these roles, we delineate a series of practice principles that must characterize the administrator and the job developer if he/she is to be effective at each of the seven stages. Maximum benefit will be gained if the reader examines this material and relates it to the material in each one of the seven stages above. After reading a chapter above, he/she should turn to the comparison material for administrators and job developers in this appendix.

The practice principles for administrators and job developers are an amalgam of actions and strategies drawn from research on human resource agencies and from human resource practitioners. These principles are specific and relevant to each of the seven stages and provide a useful guide for planning, developing, and carrying out behavioral tasks.

For the administrators and job developers at each of the seven stages, it specifies the:

(1) *operational objectives*—the specific aims or outcomes of staff performance toward which effort should be directed in order to facilitate the achievement of basic agency goals

(2) *activities*—what specifically needs to be done to achieve the operational objectives—the range of required tasks and activities to be carried out

(3) *strategies*—how the various tasks and activities should be carried out—the manner in which the tasks are to be carried out and the series of actions to be used

(4) *decisions*—the kinds of decisions or range of alternatives to be considered in carrying out the tasks and/or strategies

(5) *resources*—the kinds of resources needed to facilitate the performance of the various tasks and activities and to carry out the appropriate strategies involved in these activities.

HOW TO READ AND USE THIS APPENDIX

This appendix is set up as a reference guide and is organized to facilitate the use of its contents by administrators and job developers in human resource agencies. It is designed for a wide range of potential users—for those with a *general* interest in the division of labor among administrators and job developers involved in agency-company relationships, as well as for persons concerned with *specific* aspects of these relationships or the prescriptions for specific staff roles involved in these relationships.

The text itself begins with the *operational objectives(s)* for a specific staff role in a specific stage of the relationship. It then goes on to specify the *activities* required to achieve these objectives, the *strategies* to be used in carrying out these activities, the kinds of *decisions* to be considered during this process, and the kinds of *resources* needed to facilitate the staff member's performance of these operational procedures.

WAYS OF UTILIZING THE INFORMATION PRESENTED IN THIS SUBSECTION

The prescriptive information presented in this subsection has a number of different uses; it

(1) provides staff members in each of the agency roles with a guide for what to do, what needs to be considered, and what resources will be needed during each of the seven stages of the agency-company relationship

(2) informs the different staff members about the tasks, considerations, and needs of the other staff roles involved in the relationship

(3) allows staff members to anticipate and plan for future stages of agency-company relationships

(4) provides agency administrators and planners with a guide for what resource needs to expect and provide for during each stage of the relationship

(5) allows comparison of the prescriptions for the two staff roles *both* within a given stage and across all seven stages of the relationship

(6) provides a guide for coordinating activities during each stage of the agency-company relationship

(7) highlights the overlapping functions of various staff roles

(8) helps pinpoint some of the problem areas in agency-company relationships

(9) provides a framework on which to base the evaluation of staff performance in agency-company relationships.

ACCESS: APPROACHING THE COMPANY—STAGE I
AGENCY ADMINISTRATORS: ACCESS—STAGE I

OPERATIONAL OBJECTIVES   FOR: AGENCY ADMINISTRATORS

To open up as many companies as possible.

ACTIVITIES:

- Meet with businessmen in formal meetings to describe agency programs.
- Participate in regular activities of the business community such as the Chamber of Commerce, business luncheons, trade associations, and business conventions.
- Participate in the social life of the community such as welfare or community organizations that would provide a chance to contact businessmen informally.

STRATEGIES:

- Establish a wide range of contacts in the business community for sponsorship and information gathering.
- Establish contacts with trend-setting companies that can open the door to other companies.
- Involve key business leaders in the agency program by appointment to agency task forces or board of directors.
- Identify a business influential in each target company who has a history of interest in the activities sponsored by your agency and use him as a key informant on company organization and needs.

- Seek to establish *multiple sponsorships* from a wide range of companies and agencies.

DECISIONS

- What level of agency staff involvement is necessary at the access stage?
- Who is to be used as a contact person in the company?
- What kind of sponsorship to use in establishing initial contacts?
- Which company(ies) to develop?

RESOURCES:

- Membership in various clubs and organizations to which businessmen belong.
- Funds for special meetings, conferences, and informal social gatherings with businessmen.
- Sponsorship and introduction to social settings such as clubs and associations businessmen belong to.
- Information about specific companies both from direct contact with company personnel and public records.
  - employment structure
  - employment policy
  - employment problems
  - decision making
- Continuing information gathering within the agency about specific programs that should be communicated to businessmen.

ACCESS: APPROACHING THE COMPANY—STAGE I
JOB DEVELOPERS: ACCESS—STAGE I

OPERATIONAL OBJECTIVES   FOR: JOB DEVELOPERS

- To open up new companies for job placement.
- To provide advice, guidance, and assistance to company personnel in opening up new job opportunities for the hard-to-employ.
- To provide advice and guidance on new program development using Manpower Administration contracts.
- To lower company barriers to utilization of hard-to-employ workers.

ACTIVITIES:

- Gain access to all details and information about "opening up the company."

- Participate in selection of company to be opened up.
- Establish contacts with a broad range of company personnel.
- Develop detailed information portrait of the company employment structure.
- Scout the company and locate the decision-making gatekeepers.
- Review the manpower problems of the company with company personnel officers.

STRATEGIES:

- Identify and gain support of informal "gatekeepers" in the company.
- Attempt to establish "friendly constituencies" up and down the company hierarchy.
- Involve all levels of the company in plans to use the company for job placement.
- Work with agency in-house staff in meeting client problems, needs, and career objectives for (help in job placement).
- Use multiplier effect for new openings, that is, recruit corporate leaders from "developed" companies to use their influence with new prospects.
- Work with community-based organizations that have some influence within the company (e.g., the Chamber of Commerce).
- Identify and form coalitions with organizations that have high credibility with the company (e.g., university groups).

DECISIONS:

- What companies to open up.
- What sponsorship to seek.
- What wage and work limits to set on new job slots.
- What division of effort to set on locating jobs versus changing credentials required for jobs.

RESOURCES:

- Training in sales techniques.
- Information files on companies in the area.
- Information on receptivity of various corporate groups.
- Information on client skills.
- Information on community resources.

ENGAGEMENT: THE STRATEGY OF PENETRATION—STAGE II
AGENCY ADMINISTRATORS: ENGAGEMENT—STAGE II

OPERATIONAL OBJECTIVES   FOR: AGENCY ADMINISTRATORS

- To provide a transition from agency administrator to operating staff personnel who will develop and expand the relationship.
- To aid in the establishment of multiple contacts by operating staff workers on a number of different levels of the company.
- To keep abreast of operational progress and developments.
- To coordinate *all* agency programs that have been established within the company.

ACTIVITIES:

- Communicate with operating agency staff about overview of agency activity.
- Oversee coordination machinery that has been established between different operating units.
- Introduce operating staff to company contacts.
- Discuss agency programs with company representatives at the request of agency operating staff.
- Review each agency-company relationship periodically and regularly.
- Route communications from company personnel and other staff to operating staff who are working with the company.

STRATEGIES:

- Provide regular opportunities for staff meetings and informal contacts between *all* agency personnel who are assigned to the company to provide interchange of information.
- Establish coordination mechanisms (e.g., overlapping team structure or common membership of agency worker in all units that do business with the company).
- Disengage administrative staff from regular company contacts by transferring authority and responsibility for the agency-company relationship to operational staff as soon as possible after the company has been opened up.

DECISIONS:

- How to divide authority and responsibility among operational staff.
- What instructions and limitations to place on authority of operational staff.

- Who is to be designated as "captain" of agency contact team.
- When to withdraw administrators from the relationship.
- *How* to describe the agency program and for *what* groups in the company in order to get best reception to the work of the agency.

RESOURCES:

- Information about ongoing agency programs from agency staff.
- Information about key company contact people.
- Information about developments in companies and business organizations in the community.

ENGAGEMENT: THE STRATEGY OF PENETRATION–STAGE II
JOB DEVELOPERS: ENGAGEMENT–STAGE II

OPERATIONAL OBJECTIVES   FOR: JOB DEVELOPERS

- To aid in the establishment of multiple contacts by operating staff workers with a number of different levels of the company.
- To coordinate all job-seeking and job development efforts between the agency and the company.

ACTIVITIES:

- Update information file on company.
- Establish contacts and working relationships in many departments of the company.
- Carry out diagnosis of barriers to hiring or promotion in company (by interviewing or small group meetings).
- Meet with company representative(s).
- Analyze resources (company and agency) needed to aid agency clients.
- Develop "high support" agreement plan (what should go into it at *this* company).
  - set goals and objectives.
  - draw up schedules.
  - develop routines and procedures.
- Communicate information about contacts and planned activities to agency administrators and other operational personnel.

STRATEGIES:

- Engage in regular staff meetings (formal and informal), with all agency personnel who are assigned to the company, to provide an interchange of information.
- Act as advocate for company front-line supervisors to get them support and resources from "top dog" administrators.
- Play a supportive role to all levels of management to get them to open up the system.

DECISIONS:

- How to establish contacts with company influentials.
- How to use resources to break down barriers to employment.
- How to develop contacts and working relationships across many departments.

RESOURCES:

- Information from agency staff about ongoing agency programs.
- Information about key company contact people.
- Information about developments in companies and business organizations in the community.

NEGOTIATING A WORKING AGREEMENT—STAGE III
AGENCY ADMINISTRATORS: NEGOTIATION—STAGE III

OPERATIONAL OBJECTIVES   FOR: AGENCY ADMINISTRATORS

- To establish initially the tone of the negotiations for a working agreement.
- To act as a consultant to operational staff who carry on negotiations.
- To coordinate agency resources and personnel with company demands for service to produce a working agreement.

ACTIVITIES:

- Initiate and conclude negotiation activities.
- Ratify agreements.
- Diagnose the strategy of company negotiations.

- Disseminate and explain working agreements to all parties that will be involved in implementing the agreement.
- Provide perspectives on strategy, overall agency policy, programs, resources, and goals.

STRATEGIES:

- Remain in the wings while operational staff does the actual negotiation in order to give them greater authority and responsibility in the bargaining process.
- Involve all staff workers in the bargaining process in order that the working agreement will reflect inputs from the widest range of staff experience.
- Gain leverage for the agency by avoiding direct involvement in negotiations and retaining role as consultant and final authority to the negotiating team.

DECISIONS:

- *How* to be involved in the negotiation process.
- *When* to become involved in the negotiation process.
- *How* to best insure maximum dissemination of the details of the working agreement to company and agency staff.

RESOURCES:

- Specific information about company structure, problems, and policy.
- Information about company negotiation team.
- Information about ongoing agency operations.

NEGOTIATING A WORKING AGREEMENT—STAGE III
JOB DEVELOPERS: NEGOTIATION—STAGE III

OPERATIONAL OBJECTIVES   FOR: JOB DEVELOPERS

- To negotiate a working agreement with the company on job placement and supportive services for enrollees.
- To develop options for the negotiation staff.

ACTIVITIES:

- Participate in the negotiation process.
- Take major responsibility as spokesman for negotiation team.
- Disseminate and explain working agreement to all parties that will be involved in implementing the agreement.
- Take a coordinative role in negotiation team.

STRATEGIES:

- Involve many agency staff members in the bargaining process in order that the working agreement will reflect inputs from the widest range of staff experiences.

DECISIONS:

- How to get agreement on provisions that will give basic on-the-job support to the hard-to-employ.
- How to best insure maximum dissemination of the details of the working agreement to company and agency staff.

RESOURCES:

- Specific information about company structure, problems, and policy.
- Information about company negotiation team.
- Information about ongoing agency operations.

PROGRAM DEVELOPMENT:
STRATEGY OF SERVICE DELIVERY—STAGE IV
AGENCY ADMINISTRATORS:
PROGRAM DEVELOPMENT—STAGE IV

OPERATIONAL OBJECTIVES   FOR: AGENCY ADMINISTRATORS

- To coordinate ongoing program development activities of various operational staff members.
- To advise on program development options.

ACTIVITIES:

- Receive information about ongoing activities from various operational staff.
- Communicate information about other activities by agency staff in the same company to all operational staff.
- Schedule planning and coordination sessions to involve all operational staff who are working in a given company.
- Inform operational staff of the limits on budget and other agency resources.

STRATEGIES:

- Increase the flow of communication between various operational staff to facilitate coordination.
- Encourage meetings and coordination sessions between various operational staff working in the same company.

DECISIONS:

- The amount and kind of information to communicate to each of the operational units.
- The limits of funds, staff, and other resources to place on each relationship.

RESOURCES:

- General information about the programs, plans, and activities of each of the operational units.
- Specific information about budget, staffing, and resource needs of each of the operational units.

PROGRAM DEVELOPMENT:
STRATEGY OF SERVICE DELIVERY—STAGE IV
JOB DEVELOPER:
PROGRAM DEVELOPMENT—STAGE IV

OPERATIONAL OBJECTIVES   FOR: JOB DEVELOPERS

- To coordinate ongoing program development activities of various operational staff members.
- To advise program personnel (trainers, counselors, and so on) on content of working agreement.

- To develop and implement techniques to disseminate service plans (goals, objectives, and timetables) to a broad base of company personnel.

ACTIVITIES:

- Plan services to be given, involving all relevant company personnel in the planning process.
- Review service plans with agency administrators and company counterparts.
- Schedule work at target company *and* agency with appropriate staff assignments.
- Keep ongoing log or diary of events and history of the program (documentation).
- Maintain contact with coaches and change agent unit to reciprocally share new information on the company.
- Check with the coach to see if "high support" agreement is being fulfilled.
- Act as liaison among company personnel, clients, coaches, and agency administrators to coordinate activities and settle disputes.
- Keep continuous contact with broad range of company personnel to see if service program can be expanded.
- Arrange for supportive services program for management personnel.

STRATEGIES:

- Organize meetings and coordination sessions between various operational staff working in the same company.
- Increase the flow of communication between various operational staff to facilitate coordination.
- Involve all levels of relevant company personnel through small group conferences.

DECISIONS:

- What programs should be offered to the company.
- What the major sources of resistance to the agency programs are in the company.
- What mechanisms of coordination should be used.
- The kinds of information to communicate to each of the operational units.

RESOURCES:

- Information on company problems.
- Detailed descriptions of company programs.

- Contacts with influential members of the company executive and operational staff.
- General information about the programs, plans, and activities to each of the operational units.

THE MAINTENANCE AND EVALUATION OF
THE RELATIONSHIP—STAGE V
AGENCY ADMINISTRATORS: MAINTENANCE—STAGE V

OPERATIONAL OBJECTIVES   FOR: AGENCY ADMINISTRATORS

- To supply operational personnel with resources which they need to implement agency programs in the company.
- To coordinate the variety of ongoing operational programs in a given company.

ACTIVITIES:

- Solicit information on resource needs.
- Establish a supply and delivery schedule to insure that operational staff get needed resources on time.
- Collect information on ongoing program from operational units.
- Provide capsule summaries of ongoing programs for all operational units.
- Oversee coordination meetings involving all operational units.

STRATEGIES:

- Preplan for the resource needs of operational personnel.
- Establish ongoing coordination sessions on a regular basis to insure coordination of various operational units.

DECISION:

- What information to pass on to all operational units.
- Limits of the operating budgets of each unit.
- Extent and kind of services to provide to operational units.
- Frequency and subject matter of coordination sessions.

RESOURCES:

- General information about ongoing operational programs.
- Specific information about resource needs of operational programs.
- Extra staff, finances, service programs, educational materials, and job candidates to fill needs of operational programs.

THE MAINTENANCE AND EVALUATION OF
THE RELATIONSHIP—STAGE V
JOB DEVELOPERS: MAINTENANCE—STAGE V

OPERATIONAL OBJECTIVES   FOR: JOB DEVELOPERS

- To coordinate activities with other agency operational units.
- To provide continuous follow-up contacts and services to company personnel.
- To enlarge job placement activities for hard-to-employ clients.

ACTIVITIES:

- Keep up continuous contacts with company personnel across all departments of the company.
- Identify areas of company operations where job restructuring or counseling may be useful.
- Solicit information on company receptivity to job-related services.
- Meet regularly with other operational personnel to exchange information.

STRATEGIES:

- Establish multiple face-to-face supportive contacts with company personnel.
- Attempt to involve a broad base of company personnel in diagnosis and planning.

DECISIONS:

- How to continue and expand interest of company personnel in the job-related services.
- How to establish effective coordination machinery so that all operational personnel can optimize exchange of information and mutual support.

RESOURCES:

- General information about ongoing operational programs.
- Specific information about resource needs of operational programs.

ASSESSMENT AND EVALUATION OF
THE RELATIONSHIP–STAGE VI
AGENCY ADMINISTRATORS: ASSESSMENT–STAGE VI

OPERATIONAL OBJECTIVES   FOR: AGENCY ADMINISTRATORS

- To evaluate the effectiveness of the relationship in terms of
  - positive benefits for the hard-to-employ job candidate.
  - change in company policy procedure and structures.
  - problem solving.
  - receptivity of the company to further services.
- To learn from the relationship in order to plan future relationships.

ACTIVITIES:

- Gather information on original goals and their implementation.
- Compile a historical story line of the relationship.
- Consult with all operational staff about the relationship, probing for best and worst features.
- Discuss impact of relationship with company personnel.

STRATEGIES:

- Compare original goals of the agency with actual outcomes of the relationship.
- Evaluate extent to which agreements with the company were fulfilled.
- Assess impact of agency services on company programs, structures, and policies toward the hard-to-employ.
- Probe for company's willingness to continue or expand the relationship with the agency.

DECISIONS:

- The extent to which the agency fulfilled its responsibility to carry out agreed on services.

- The extent of the impact of agency programs on company structure and programs for the hard-to-employ.
- Reasons for problems in agency service delivery.
- Alternative methods that could have been used by the agency in the relationship.
- Ways to improve future relationships with companies.
- Extent to which agency can provide continued service to the company.

RESOURCES:

- General information on the relationship from all operational units.
- Specific information on special problems or good points in the relationship.
- Specific process records of all operational staff.
- All written documents about the relationship.
- Statistics on company hiring procedures and policies.
- Interviews with selected company personnel.

ASSESSMENT AND EVALUATION OF
THE RELATIONSHIP—STAGE VI
JOB DEVELOPERS: ASSESSMENT—STAGE VI

OPERATIONAL OBJECTIVES   FOR: JOB DEVELOPERS

- To advise agency administrators on the course of operational activities by the job developers in the company.
- To evaluate the impact of job development activities on the hard-to-employ in the company.
- To learn from the relationship in order to plan future relationships.

ACTIVITIES:

- Gather information on original goals and their implementation.
- Consult with all operational staff about the relationship, probing for best and worst features.
- Discuss impact of relationship with company personnel.

STRATEGIES:

- Compare original goals of the agency with actual outcome of the relationship.
- Evaluate extent to which agreements with the company were fulfilled.

- Assess impact of agency services on company programs, structures and policies toward the hard-to-employ.
- Probe for company's willingness to continue to expand the relationship with the agency.

DECISIONS:

- The extent to which the agency fulfilled its responsibility to carry out agreed on services.
- The extent of the impact of agency programs on company structure and programs for the hard-to-employ.
- Reasons for problems in agency service delivery.
- Alternative methods that could have been used by the agency in the relationship.
- Ways to improve future relationships with companies.
- Extent to which agency can provide continued service to the company.

RESOURCES:

- General information on the relationship from all operational units.
- Specific information on special problems or good points in the relationship.
- Specific process records of all operational staff.
- All written documents about the relationship.
- Statistics on company hiring procedures and policies.
- Interviews with selected company personnel.

DISENGAGEMENT: THE STRATEGY OF WITHDRAWAL—STAGE VII
AGENCY ADMINISTRATORS: DISENGAGEMENT—STAGE VII

OPERATIONAL OBJECTIVES   FOR: AGENCY ADMINISTRATORS

- To disengage from the agency-company relationship.
- To insure that the products of past agency services continue to have some impact on company operations.
- To leave open the door for the resumption and/or continuation of some agency services to the company.

ACTIVITIES:

- Discuss the pros and cons of ending the relationship with all staff members who are engaged in servicing the company.

- Discuss the pros and cons of disengagement with company personnel who have been involved in the service program.
- Seek alternative relationships or areas of service that will continue to involve agency and company personnel in a working agreement.
- Develop and present alternative programs of service in conjunction with operational staff which would prevent complete termination of contact with the company.
- Set up a series of exit interviews at all levels of company with joint analysis and planning of how program outcomes may be maintained.
- Communicate to "top dog" company officials the history of the agency-company relationship, particularly, its strengths, weaknesses, and outcomes.

STRATEGIES:

- Conduct discussions of disengagement with representatives of the company in a manner which leaves a number of doors open for future relationships.
- Seek to streamline the service program by disengaging from less effective operations and strengthening effective operations.
- Provide additional service opportunities while curtailing existing programs.
- Seek to provide technical assistance that will make it possible for the agency service to become part of "normal" company practices.
- Try to interest the company in hiring or borrowing agency staff to develop do-it-yourself programs.

DECISIONS:

- Whether to terminate all contact with a company.
- What is the extent of a continued relationship, if any?
- How much importance to give to views of operational staff about disengagement?
- Which alternative programs to use in continuing the relationship with the company?
- Amount of resources to devote to a continued relationship.
- How to revise agency programs and procedures in light of the outcome of the relationship?

RESOURCES:

- Information on company service needs.
- Information on company satisfaction or dissatisfaction with agency programs.

- Programs of alternative services which would be offered to the company including:
  - Educational.
  - Staff development.
  - Training.
  - Placement.
- Funds, new staff, and new formats for new service delivery programs.

DISENGAGEMENT: THE STRATEGY OF WITHDRAWAL–STAGE VII
JOB DEVELOPERS: DISENGAGEMENT–STAGE VII

OPERATIONAL OBJECTIVES   FOR: JOB DEVELOPERS

- To disengage from the agency-company relationship.
- To insure that the products of past agency services continue to have some impact on company operations.
- To leave open the door for the resumption and/or continuation of some agency services to the company.

ACTIVITIES:

- Discuss the pros and cons of ending the relationship with agency administrators who are responsible for servicing the company.
- Discuss the pros and cons of disengagement with company personnel who have been involved in the service program.
- Seek alternative relationships or areas of service that will continue to involve agency and company personnel in a working agreement.
- Develop and present alternative programs of service in conjunction with operational staff which would prevent complete termination of contact with the company.
- To integrate innovative employment practices into normal company operations and procedures.
- To work with company personnel to build for the future support and maintenance of employment innovations after agency personnel have departed.

STRATEGIES:

- Conduct discussions of disengagement with representative of the company in a manner which leaves a number of doors open for future relationships.
- Provide additional service opportunities while curtailing existing programs.

- Seek to provide technical assistance that will make it possible for the agency service to become part of "normal" company practices.
- Try to interest the company in hiring or borrowing agency staff to develop do-it-yourself programs.

DECISIONS:

- Whether to terminate all contact with a company.
- What is to be the extent of a continued relationship, if any?
- How much importance to give to the views of operational staff about disengagement?
- Which alternative programs to use in continuing the relationship with the company?
- Amount of resources to devote to a continued relationship.
- How to revise agency programs and procedures in light of the outcome of the relationship?

RESOURCES:

- Information on company service needs.
- Information on company satisfaction or dissatisfaction with agency programs.
- Programs of alternative services which could be offered to the company including:
  - Educational.
  - Staff development.
  - Training.
  - Placement.
- Funds, new staff, and new formats for new service delivery programs.

ABOUT THE AUTHORS

LOUIS A. FERMAN is research director of the Institute of Labor and Industrial Relations of the University of Michigan and professor of social work at that university. He has published numerous articles and books on manpower development for the hard-to-employ. His latest books are *Job Development for the Hard-to-Employ, Negroes and Jobs,* and *Poverty in America.* He has conducted more than 75 training workshops for professionals in the manpower field.

ROGER MANELA holds Master's degrees in Social Work and Sociology from the University of Michigan, and is presently completing a doctoral dissertation on how men and women cope with divorce. Formerly a Research Associate at the University of Michigan's Schools of Social Work and Public Health, he is presently associated with the University of Michigan's Program for Urban Health Research.

DAVID ROGERS is a senior member of Service Innovations Corporation, a Chicago-based training and consulting firm specializing in services to human service organizations. His principal work has been in areas of client treatment and processing, job development, placement, and postplacement client support. A contributor to employment and training handbooks produced by the University of Michigan's Institute of Labor and Industrial Relations, he also coauthored *Coaching in a Manpower Program* and *A Practical Guide to Employing the Low-Skilled, Disadvantaged Worker* for the U.S. Department of Labor. He also serves as a lecturer in manpower and human resources development in the graduate Public Administration Program at Roosevelt University.